THE ORIGINAL ZODIAC

"Graham Phillips adds a whole new dimension to the world of Göbekli Tepe by showing that behind all the incredible carved art and animal reliefs lies a cohesive system that could well be the beginnings of astrology as we know it. This is an important addition to the ancient mysteries bookshelf."

ANDREW COLLINS, AUTHOR OF
KARAHAN TEPE AND *GÖBEKLI TEPE*

"This thoroughly researched book reveals, for the first time to the modern world, the earliest known form of astrology and its zodiac, with roots in the world's oldest known temple complex, Göbekli Tepe. A groundbreaking work."

DEBORAH BENSTEAD, AUTHOR OF
THE INWARD REVOLUTION

"For decades Graham Phillips has consistently produced remarkable, fresh insights into subjects of perennial interest such as the Ark of the Covenant and the Holy Grail. To give us something new on the zodiac and astrology that combines recent scientific research with ancient history is worthy of note. To make it compellingly readable makes it all the more so."

PAUL WESTON, AUTHOR OF
ALEISTER CROWLEY AND THE AEON OF HORUS AND
THE MICHAEL LINE, THE QABALAH AND THE TAROT

"Having known Graham for more than 30 years, I can say he is one of the most conscientious and thorough researchers in the esoteric history world. If he says there are grounds to consider a new, groundbreaking theory or concept, you can take it to the bank. Graham Phillips is always ahead of the curve and has been for years! He is a true pioneer of esoteric history, research, and exploration."

Mark Ryan, author of *Hold Fast* and coauthor of *The Greenwood Tarot* and *The Wildwood Tarot*

THE ORIGINAL ZODIAC

What Ancient Astrology Reveals About You

GRAHAM PHILLIPS

Bear & Company
Rochester, Vermont

Bear & Company
One Park Street
Rochester, Vermont 05767
www.BearandCompanyBooks.com

Text stock is SFI certified

Bear & Company is a division of Inner Traditions International

Cataloging-in-Publication Data for this title is available from the Library of Congress

ISBN 978-1-59143-541-9 (print)
ISBN 978-1-59143-542-6 (ebook)

Printed and bound in the United States by Lake Book Manufacturing, LLC
The text stock is SFI certified. The Sustainable Forestry Initiative® program promotes sustainable forest management.

10 9 8 7 6 5 4 3 2 1

Text design Virginia Scott Bowman and layout by Debbie Glogover
This book was typeset in Garamond Premier Pro with Bruphy Trial, Gelica, Gill Sans MT Pro, and Kepler Std used as display typefaces
Artwork by Graham Phillips

To send correspondence to the author of this book, mail a first-class letter to the author c/o Inner Traditions • Bear & Company, One Park Street, Rochester, VT 05767, and we will forward the communication, or contact the author directly at **grahamphillips.net**.

CONTENTS

THE ANCIENT SIGNS

NEW EVIDENCE FOR ASTROLOGY

This book uncovers the original 18-sign zodiac, an ancient system that predates the familiar 12-sign zodiac by millennia. However, before examining the discoveries that led to the reconstruction of this remarkable long-lost astrological system, we present groundbreaking scientific evidence supporting a fundamental principle of astrology—that the timing of one's birth can significantly influence one's character and personality. The ancients, it seems, were right. Birth signs really do shape who we are.

The zodiac is an imaginary band of sky surrounding the Earth divided into 12 equal sections, each named after the corresponding constellations or patterns of stars within them, which astrologers call signs. Namely, Aries, Taurus, Gemini, Cancer, Leo, Virgo, Libra, Scorpio, Sagittarius, Capricorn, Aquarius, and Pisces. While there are a total of 88 constellations, including 76 others like Orion, Pegasus, and the Great Bear, the zodiac is of particular significance for astrology because the sun, moon, and all the planets seem to only move within it as they travel across the heavens. The reason is that they all orbit very closely to the same plane around the sun, and the moon moves along a similar plane while orbiting Earth. In astronomical terms, this plane is known as the ecliptic, and the zodiac covers a zone extending approximately 8.5 degrees to either side.

Astrologers believe that the relative positions of celestial bodies in the zodiac, particularly the sun, can influence a person's destiny. The zodiac sign occupied by the sun at the time of someone's birth—called their sun, star, or birth sign—is believed to play a significant role in shaping their characteristics and personality. It is also thought that the positions of the sun, moon, and planets at a specific moment can similarly influence the lives of individuals born under the same sign. A diagram charting these positions is called a horoscope, a word synonymous with regular media columns predicting readers' astrological fate and fortune. Despite living in a scientific and technological era, millions worldwide continue to trust in the accuracy of their birth signs, and many frequently seek guidance from their horoscopes. So, is there any hard evidence that astrology works?

Over the years, several statistical research projects have been undertaken to examine astrology, and their findings have been thought-provoking. Many of these studies have found that astrological birth signs are significantly more accurate than would be expected by chance alone. The first was the work of the French statisticians Françoise and Michel Gauquelin, who, between the 1950s and 80s, meticulously studied the profiles of thousands of athletes, actors, and scientists and concluded a remarkable correlation between their birth signs and their accomplishments.[1] While the Gauquelins' findings initially faced criticism, many, including the esteemed psychologist Hans Eysenck, eventually supported their results. Other such studies have since had similar results. Skeptics, however, continue to doubt that astrology has any realistic basis. But now, advancements in cell biology and understanding of life's intricate responses to seasonal rhythms are revealing compelling new evidence suggesting sun signs might have a firm scientific foundation.

The Case for Sun Signs

The ancient Greeks devised the 12-sign zodiac we know today. Sun signs such as Leo, Virgo, and Libra were the locations in the zodiac where the sun appeared to be, as seen from Earth at a given time. They couldn't see the constellation directly because of the sun's glare, but they could work it out by seeing what zodiac constellations were visible after dark. The

ancient new year began around what would now be March 21, the spring equinox in the northern hemisphere, and as Aries was the sign the sun was in at that time, it was considered the first sign, followed by Taurus, Gemini, and so on. As every sign took up precisely 30 degrees of the zodiac, the solar stay in each one was almost 30 and a half days, which was awkward, so it was simplified into most signs having 30 or 31 days, while three of them had one more or one less. Accordingly, between March 21 and April 19, it would be Aries; April 20 and May 20, Taurus; May 21 and June 20, Gemini; and so on, just as the astrological signs are today. The zodiac is, therefore, a celestial calendar, and the sun sign indicates the time of year. Maybe the stars are too far away to influence someone's characteristics and personality, but perhaps the *time of year* during which pregnancy occurs does have an influence.

Earth spins on its axis, causing night and day; it also moves about the sun in an orbit, taking just over 365 days or one year. If the Earth rotated around an axis inclined at 90 degrees to its orbital plane around the Sun—in other words, upright—day and night would be of equal length, and there would also be no seasons. However, its axis is tilted by approximately 23.5 degrees, meaning that when the planet is on one side of the sun, the northern hemisphere is pointed toward it and the south away, and six months later, the opposite occurs. There are longer days, more warmth, and more sunlight in the hemisphere pointing toward the sun, hence summer, and less when pointing away, therefore winter. And the seasons gradually alternate between the two. The overall result is the dramatic, annual cycle of nature.

Plant growth patterns, such as blossoming in spring, fruiting in summer, and shedding leaves in autumn, are synchronized with the seasons. Animals also exhibit seasonal changes: hibernation in winter, spring breeding, and fall migration are just a few ways the animal kingdom responds to the seasons. Known as chronobiology, such changes are controlled by hormones, chemicals that coordinate various functions by carrying messages telling the body what to do.[2] And the same circannual rhythms, as they are called, also occurred in our remote ancestors.[3] Remarkably, it is now known that they still do. Although circannual rhythms are less evident in modern humans, as we have considerable artificial control over our environment, modern research has shown that seasonal hormonal changes still occur—and to a significant degree.[4] A recent study by the Department of Molecular Cell Biology at the Weizmann Institute of Science in Israel, published in 2021 in the prestigious *Proceedings of the National Academy of Sciences*, presents persuasive evidence that humans have hormonal rhythms that may significantly influence our circannual physiology, far more than previously thought.

The team used a dataset of millions of hormone tests from medical records that revealed previously unsuspected seasonality variations in hormones for numerous functions, such as reproduction, growth, metabolism, and stress adaptation. For example, hormones from the pituitary gland, which help control reproduction, metabolism, stress, and lactation, peaked in August. Peripheral organs under the control of the pituitary, like those that produce sex hormones or the thyroid hormone, showed seasonality in February. Meanwhile, testosterone produced by the adrenal gland, estradiol produced by the ovaries, and progesterone produced by the adrenal cortex reached their pinnacle in May, and the pituitary hormone ACTH peaked in October. As these hormonal changes gradually transformed over the year, in many cases it was even possible to tell the month of the year that a blood sample was taken without consulting the relevant record.[5]

The Weizmann Institute findings explains why people born at the same time of the year share specific psychological and physiological characteristics. It is well known that the levels of various hormones in the mother's system play a significant part in fetal development. So, if hormones change regularly throughout the year and have an annual rhythm, the pregnancy timing could considerably affect the child's eventual physiological and psychological characteristics.[6] Although the environment after birth influences our personality, many of our general character traits are determined by genetics, which can be modified by such hormonal changes as this study has revealed.[7] In other words, individuals who spent the same period of the year in the womb would be affected similarly and be born around the same date. Circannual hormonal changes may account for the apparent accuracy of astrology, so from the biological perspective, it's not the stars shaping our destiny but the period during the year we spend in the womb. Someone born in a particular sun sign would usually have undergone fetal development during the same months as another born in the same sign and consequently would have experienced similar hormonal influences. It seems, at last, that there is a scientific case for people being born at the same time of the year sharing common characteristics. Which, after all, is what sun signs are all about.

THE ORIGINAL ZODIAC

The Greek Zodiac

The zodiac we know today was devised by the Greeks around 300 BCE. Each of its 12 signs shares a name with a stellar constellation. But how did they get their names? They are not recognizable in the pictorial sense. Who could claim, for example, that the Y-shaped arrangement of stars that form the Cancer constellation in any way resembles a crab or that the line of stars forming Aries remotely resembles a ram? The stars that fall in each sign could be joined by lines to make any conceivable shape. Indeed, throughout history, separate cultures have imagined the stars to form very different patterns in the sky. For example, the Egyptians regarded the stars of Taurus as a turtle,[1] the Chinese saw Virgo as a horn,[2] and the Mayans envisaged Aquarius as a bat.[3] Well, it was for astrological rather than astronomical reasons.

The signs were chosen not for the constellation's resemblance to what they were named after but for the symbolic qualities they represented. Ancient astrologers believed that birth dates shaped human characteristics, and the zodiac sector in which the sun was present at birth was deemed responsible. The sign was, therefore, named after a creature or mythical figure that best symbolized the character and personality traits of those born in the sign, and its stars eventually incorporated into the associated pictorial image. For example, someone

born with the sun in Aries was not considered to have inherited ram-like qualities because the constellation looked anything like a ram; the ram was chosen as an image for the sign once ram-like qualities had been observed in people born at that time of year. Similarly, a person born during the sign of Leo was not thought to have inherited lion-like qualities from the constellation; the lion was chosen after lion-like qualities had been observed in people born when the sun was in that sector of the zodiac. The same applies to the signs symbolized by mythical figures rather than animals. Their attributes were similarly considered to epitomize those born in the sign named after them. Aquarius, the water carrier, was the romantic hero Ganymede; Virgo, the maiden, was Astraea, goddess of precision; Libra, the scales, was the symbol for Themis, the goddess of justice; Sagittarius, the archer, was the benevolent centaur Chiron; and Gemini, the twins, were the adventuring Argonauts Castor and Pollux.[4]

The Mesopotamian Zodiac

The ancient Greeks did not invent the zodiac concept; they were influenced by the Babylonians. Ancient Babylon was a thriving city-state in Mesopotamia, located near the Euphrates River in present-day Iraq. It emerged as a cultural and political powerhouse during the reign of Hammurabi (1792–1750 BCE), who is renowned for the Code of Hammurabi, one of the earliest written legal codes. Babylon became a hub of innovation, trade, and governance, blending Sumerian, Akkadian, and Semitic influences. The city reached its zenith under King Nebuchadnezzar II (605–562 BCE). His architectural achievements included the famed Hanging Gardens, one of the Seven Wonders of the Ancient World, and the magnificent Ishtar Gate. These symbolized Babylon's wealth and architectural prowess. The ziggurat of Etemenanki, believed to inspire the biblical Tower of Babel, demonstrated their dedication to religion and astronomy. Babylon was a center of learning, contributing to advancements in mathematics, astronomy, and literature. It is home to the Epic of Gilgamesh, one of the oldest surviving literary works.[5]

The Babylonians had an earlier version of the 12-sign zodiac, which included signs of familiar creatures like a bull, crab, and lion and different animals such as a swallow, wolf, and swan. Indeed, all these earlier signs were named after animals, which is why they were collectively called the *zodiac.*[6] Our modern word comes from the Greek *zodiakós kýklos*, meaning "cycle of animals." Only later were five of the animals replaced with Hellenic symbolism that confusingly now bears the Latin names Aquarius, Virgo, Libra, Sagittarius, and Gemini.[7]

The history of the zodiac goes back further. Babylon had existed for two millennia before they adopted this 12-sign zodiac; their earlier astrologers employed a very different one with 18 signs. It is known from various fragmentary texts, but the oldest complete description survives on a clay tablet dating from 686 BCE found during excavations of the ancient city of Nineveh in Mosul, northern Iraq.[8] Now in the British Museum and cataloged as BM 86378, the text references all the signs without directly revealing which stars they were associated with, except the first. It is referred to as the Star Cluster, identified as what is now called the Pleiades, or the Seven Sisters, a close grouping of stars in the constellation of Taurus, which they called the Spider.

This first sign began on the spring equinox and was followed by the others, each representing 20 degrees of the zodiac. The BM 86378 text reveals that they were symbolized by animals, some of this symbolism surviving until Greek times, with such signs as the Lion, the Scorpion, and the Bull. However, they were originally denoted by different stars, ascribed to other sectors in the zodiac band, and concerned different times of the year to the modern zodiac. The tablet alone does not clarify some of these, having names like The Great One, the god Pabilsaĝ, and the goddess Annunitum. Fortunately, they can be established by other surviving texts included in over 30,000 inscribed clay tablets found in 1851 during excavations of Nineveh by the English archeologist Austen Layard. Dating from the seventh century BCE, they include various astronomical texts from which the imagery of the early zodiac signs can be determined. Like the later 12-sign Babylonian zodiac, they were all represented by animals.[9] They are, in order: Spider,

Map of ancient Mesopotamia showing important sites and modern countries.

Orox, Mouflon, Vulture, Gazelle, Serpent, Crayfish, Lion, Swan, Crane, Scorpion, Horse, Goat, Wolf, Fish, Swallow, Eagle, and Fox.

Astonishingly, the BM 86378 tablet also reveals that this 18-sign zodiac must have been devised well before the Babylonians. It all concerns a planetary phenomenon termed *axial precession.* Also called the precession of the equinoxes, axial precession is the slow and continuous change in the Earth's rotational axis. Imagine a straight bar through the planet, sticking out into space on either side at the north and south poles. During axial precession, although the bar remains at an angle of approximately 23.5 away from upright, each end traces a complete circle through space roughly every 26,000 years. Accordingly, every 2,166 years, the sun appears to move back a sign.[10]

When the Greeks created their zodiac around 2300 years ago, between March 21 and April 19—what we now consider Aries—the sun was indeed in the zodiac segment dominated by the Aries constellation. However, today, between those dates, the sun is now in the zodiac sector dominated by the constellation Pisces. The same applies to every sign: they have all moved back one. What had been Taurus is now Aries, what was Gemini is now Taurus, what was Cancer is now Gemini, and so on.[11] If you have doubts, check an online planetarium. Enter your date of birth and see which constellations the sun is in—it will be the one before your familiar sign. But if you swear by your birth sign, there's no need to worry. As far as astrology is concerned, anyone born in the 30 days following the spring equinox is nevertheless born in the zodiac sector symbolized by the ram—precisely like in ancient Greece—it's just that the sun is now in the 30-degree zodiac segment dominated by the Pisces constellation. The same goes for all the signs. (Remember, it's the time of the year you were born that is thought to determine human characteristics and character traits, not the stars with which the sun aligns.) Which brings us back to the BM 86378 tablet.

As mentioned, the constellation referred to as the Star Cluster, the Spider, is identified as the Pleiades. Aries is the first sign of the Greek zodiac because it was created around 300 BCE when the sun was in the Aries constellation at the spring equinox. If the 18-sign zodiac was contrived when the sun was near the Pleiades constellation at the spring equinox, it had to have been devised millennia before the Babylonian civilization arose. Because of axial precession, the last time the sun was close to the Pleiades at that time of year was some 7,000 years ago.[12] This means that for the Pleiades to have been the first sign, this 18-sign zodiac must have been compiled as long ago as 5000 BCE. This is over 2,000 years before the building of Stonehenge and the pyramids of Egypt, making it, by far, the oldest known zodiac devised anywhere in the world. (Again, you can check this with any online planetarium. Enter March 21, 5000 BCE, and you'll see the sun next to the Pleiades.) Amazingly, this 18-sign zodiac may be even older.

Babylon was in a region known as Mesopotamia, a stretch of fertile land between the Tigris and Euphrates rivers, extending from the Persian Gulf in the south of Iraq to southeast Turkey in the north. Seven thousand years ago, the area was inhabited by a Neolithic farming culture called the Samarra.[13] Unfortunately, they had no form of writing, so we know little about their astrological beliefs. However, evidence concerning their zodiac seems to exist with their predecessors, the mysterious people who built Göbekli Tepe. Situated in southeastern Turkey, Göbekli Tepe is a megalithic complex that appears to have been, like other ancient monuments such as Stonehenge, part temple, part astronomical observatory. However, it is far more extensive and much older. Created over 11,000 years ago, Göbekli Tepe comprises 20 circular compounds each up to 65 feet in diameter, consisting of around 200 T-shaped stone pillars each up to 18 feet high and weighing as much as 20 tons.[14] These pillars are intricately carved with animal figures, many thought to symbolize stellar constellations. However, because the builders left no writings, it is unknown which stars they represented or how these ancient people interpreted them. Nevertheless, 14 of the animals of the 18-sign zodiac are prominently carved onto the stones of Göbekli Tepe. The only signs we don't see are the Crayfish, the Fish, the Swan, and the Swallow, but even two of these may be represented: a zig-zag, chevron design found on one of the pillars may be the swan goddess Nisaba, and the Fish might be represented by a large fishing net carved on another. Some of the Göbekli Tepe figures are no longer identifiable, so it is entirely possible that a crayfish and swallow were amongst them.[15]

So, this 18-sign zodiac is thousands of years older than the one we are familiar with today. We don't know what specific stars were incorporated into constellations to represent each of these ancient signs. Still, we know that the list began at the spring equinox and that the subsequent year was divided into 18 divisions of some 20 days each. These, therefore, appear to be the sacred creatures of the original Mesopotamian zodiac, with the dates covered by each birth sign.

As we have seen, modern astrological belief holds that the Aries sign still influences those born in late March or early April, even though the sun is now in Pisces at that time. Similarly, it makes no difference that today, the sun is nowhere near the Pleiades until late May. If we use the original Mesopotamian zodiac, someone born in the 20 days beginning March 21 would still be born in the Spider sign, and the same goes for all the other signs. Accordingly, the chart on page 12 still reveals your Mesopotamian birth sign.

THE MESOPOTAMIAN ZODIAC

Position	Sign	Date Range
1	Spider	March 21–April 9
2	Orox	April 10–May 3
3	Mouflon	May 4–May 21
4	Vulture	May 22–June 10
5	Gazelle	June 11–July 1
6	Serpent	July 2–July 20
7	Crayfish	July 21–August 10
8	Lion	August 11–August 30
9	Swan	August 31–September 20
10	Crane	September 21–October 11
11	Scorpion	October 12–November 4
12	Horse	November 5–November 24
13	Goat	November 25–December 12
14	Wolf	December 13–December 23
15	Fish	December 24–January 14
16	Swallow	January 15–February 7
17	Eagle	February 8–March 1
18	Fox	March 2–March 20

Just as Greek and Roman mythology informed their interpretation of the zodiac, so did that of the Mesopotamians. The oldest known cultures in the region were those that built Göbekli Tepe and the Samarra people. Still, as they had no form of writing, their beliefs can only be gleaned from the records of their successors, the Sumerians, Akkadians, Babylonians, and Assyrians, beginning around 3000 BCE. From their ancient surviving literary works, such as the Epic of Gilgamesh, we learn that their chief deities included the sky god Anu, Enlil, the god of air and storms, and Enki, the god of wisdom and water. These gods were seen as powerful yet humanlike, with emotions, desires, and conflicts that shaped the fate of humanity.[16] However, most Mesopotamian gods were either depicted as animals or had an animal with which they were associated, and these were the creatures incorporated into the original zodiac. Many of their names are still unknown, but the known ones included in the zodiac are the pastoral deity Amurru, whose sacred animal was the gazelle; the grain goddess Nisaba, depicted as a swan; Pabilsaĝ, a hunter deity epitomized by a pony-like wild horse; Gula, goddess of healing symbolized by a dog or wolf; Annunitum, the goddess of love and war represented by an eagle; and Anu symbolized by the mouflon or wild sheep.[17]

No record survives concerning how this original zodiac was interpreted or what character traits were associated with each sign. However, that doesn't mean it can't be reconstructed today. If aspects of someone's character and personality are genuinely influenced by the time of year—hence, in which of these ancient signs—they were born, then a statistical survey should reveal shared traits. And it does. Over several years, I compiled an in-depth survey, recording people's attitudes, opinions, likes, dislikes, hobbies, pastimes, employment, health, and many other factors, and found that those born in each sign did appear to share common traits well beyond what should be expected by chance. What follows is inspired by that research. This is the ancient Mesopotamian zodiac—the original zodiac—revealing, for the first time in millennia, the personality and character traits shared by those born in each of its signs. It is in no way intended to challenge conventional astrology. Instead, it is an alternative and equally fascinating interpretation of ancient birth signs in a format relevant to today's world.

THE ANCIENT SIGNS

SPIDER

★ ★ ★

March 21–April 9

The spider is a solitary creature with the remarkable ability to create an extraordinary web. Likewise, those born in this sign are independent and highly creative thinkers known for their exceptional blend of imagination and practicality. Spiders have a grounded perspective, constantly evaluating their path to ensure they are on the right track. One of the defining Spider traits is their insatiable curiosity concerning the world around them. They are recognized for their analytical nature and inclination for self-reflection, which can sometimes border on the overcritical. Spiders can achieve outstanding results quickly; their success is often attributed to their charm, tact, and willingness to assist others.

Spiders, despite their ever-changing interests and strategies, may exhibit leadership qualities. However, their adaptability can sometimes leave followers feeling left behind. This isn't due to insensitivity but rather is a testament to their ability to adjust to new circumstances. Spiders naturally assume others will do the same, often underestimating the effect of their changes in direction on those around them. Despite their interest in the arts, Spiders rarely enjoy traditional forms of entertainment like concerts or theatre, preferring to create their own. This independent spirit is a hallmark of the Spider sign. Those born in this cycle value the present more than the past, focusing on today rather than dwelling on yesterday, and are seldom ones to hold on to keepsakes or memorabilia. They have realistic expectations in relationships and are willing to work for a long and happy partnership. If a relationship ends, they show resilience and move on without holding grudges, viewing breakups not as rejection but as part of life's journey.

Although somewhat fussy or faddy, people born in the Spider sign are good socializers. At ease in company, they have an entertaining personality and a versatile character, making them the soul of any party. However, Spiders often give the impression that they do not quite share the spirit of the occasion. It is not that they are rude or uninterested; instead, they are usually thinking of more than one thing at once.

The Spider is generally neat and somewhat obsessive about cleanliness in domestic life. However, although they know exactly where everything is, their personal space tends to be a complete mess. Nevertheless, Spiders are often overconcerned with cleanliness, and many are hypochondriacs, worried that the slightest ailment is the start of serious illness.

The Spider processes information like a computer, organizing even the most disordered data into clear and coherent categories. They are perfectionists, which can lead to problems if they expect others to apply themselves similarly. Spiders work best alone. Although those born in this sign can be somewhat self-centered, they are generous and helpful and make excellent and entertaining friends. The Spider is intelligent, clever, and resourceful but is inclined to go their way, ignoring the advice of others until mistakes are made. Spiders can have an unusual, sometimes zany, and somewhat random sense of humor. Some people find them hilarious, while others don't get them at all. They have many friends and are prepared to take the lead in most situations. Being excellent communicators, they are unafraid of public speaking and make ideal lecturers, teachers, and salespeople.

One of the most notable traits of the person born in this sign is their ability to change their character and mannerisms to suit a situation, which can make them exceptional actors and performers. Spiders tend to be extroverted, noisy, and rapid movers, finding it difficult to stay still. Although intelligent and quick to learn, they can lose interest when trained by others and work best when self-taught.

The Spider represents one of the swiftest signs, and those born in this zodiac cycle can rapidly progress. However, they have numerous leisure activities and spend too much time enjoying themselves. Additionally, Spiders are extravagant, not the best economizers, and spend more than they can realistically afford. All the same, the Spider can be one of the most generous, entertaining, and engaging partners and friends.

Positive Characteristics

The Spider has great versatility. Endowed with an alert mind and an excellent memory, they can solve many problems that others find difficult. Those born in this sign are especially precise regarding minute detail; intelligent and creative, they take pride in their work. In business, they work best alone and are capable of long periods of devoted activity. Philosophical interests are a marked feature, with considerable originality of ideas. Erudite and persuasive, the Spider is a natural entertainer with a marvelous sense of humor. They have a great memory and can recall detailed information that often surprises those around them. People of this sign are swift, decisive, spontaneous, and imaginative and can quickly accomplish much. They are usually kind and have considerable affinity with animals. One of the most striking qualities of Spiders is their meticulous nature. Another notable characteristic is their analytical mind. Spiders possess solid problem-solving abilities, allowing them to dissect complex issues and find practical solutions. Those born under the sign of the Spider are known for their remarkable creativity and excel at critical thinking. They possess a natural talent for weaving together complex ideas and finding unique solutions, making them excellent strategists and innovators. Their patience allows them to excel in tasks requiring precision and foresight. Spiders are also deeply intuitive, often sensing underlying truths and motives that others might miss. Their adaptability enables them to thrive in various environments and situations. Loyal and protective, they build strong, lasting relationships, creating a close-knit circle of trusted allies.

Negative Characteristics

If an enterprise fails, the Spider may become oversensitive and quick to take offense. Pessimism is usual for Spiders who have suffered a setback, and their response is generally to withdraw, accepting further problems as if they somehow deserve them. Although critical of themselves, they dislike being criticized by others and are usually the last people to take advice. Extravagance and impatience can lead to financial problems. Those born in this sign can be overimaginative and get involved in impractical endeavors. Their love of adventure can lead to too much time being spent away from the more practical aspects of life. Spiders can be worriers and often suffer from anxiety if they are not kept active. They can be escapists who tend to avoid responsibilities in a world of their own making. Their meticulous nature can lead to perfectionism, making them overly critical of themselves and others. This tendency can cause them to focus excessively on minor flaws, leading to stress and dissatisfaction. Spiders can also be overly analytical, sometimes overthinking situations and struggling to make decisions. Their strong sense of duty may make them inflexible, resistant to change, and overly cautious. Additionally, their modesty can sometimes turn into self-doubt, making it hard to acknowledge their achievements and maintain confidence in their abilities.

Appearance

Spiders usually have an upright appearance and smooth complexion with warm, attractive eyes. Often large, the eyes are commonly the most striking feature of the Spider. Those born in this sign tend to be slim with sharp or angular features and often retain a youthful appearance well into middle age. Even the worry lines that may appear on their faces make them look wiser rather than older. Although not particularly interested in fashion, those born in this zodiac cycle have a good dress sense and often look best in neutral colors such as black, white, gray, or brown. Spiders are quick movers with fast actions, and many are inclined to fidget, mainly when concentrating. They are usually erudite, good speakers who prefer to talk rather than sit and listen.

Health

The body parts readily prone to infection are the stomach and abdomen; indigestion and intestinal difficulties are invariably complaints for those born in this sign. Stress and anxiety are typical symptoms for Spiders, who may benefit from relaxation techniques like meditation. Nervous disorders may also be in evidence, and hypochondria is common. Strangely enough, the Spider is often the bravest regarding genuine illness. If they fall sick or face injury, they cope well and may even continue their routine against medical advice. However, the Spider is a sign of good health; those born in this cycle are usually fit and trim. They typically follow balanced diets and exercise routines, and their attention to detail helps them maintain good health and fitness habits.

The Formula for Success

The Spider is a highly versatile creature regarding social interactions and business affairs. Their natural humor and acting abilities enable them to seamlessly adapt to various situations, resulting in high levels of success. One of their most remarkable talents is bringing out the best in others, infusing even the most mundane tasks with interest and enthusiasm. Possessing considerable charisma and exceptionally creative minds, Spiders often generate unconventional and original ideas, albeit drawing criticism from less imaginative people. Nevertheless, Spiders are known for rising to the occasion and proving their skeptics wrong. Analytical prowess is a hallmark trait of the Spider, and individuals born under this sign excel at solving even the most complex problems. Their vivid imaginations make them excellent teachers, entertainers, and performers, showcasing their ability to persuade and influence others to see things from their perspective. The Spider's loyalty and sense of responsibility make them trustworthy friends and partners. Additionally, they possess compassion and a desire to help others, often putting others' needs before theirs.

Words of Advice

The Spider should focus on one task at a time rather than on numerous problems simultaneously. Their most significant drawback is that they have too many interests, ideas, and skills to devote themselves sufficiently to a single project. Their hypercritical side badly needs controlling, as does their touchiness about being criticized themselves. Generally sensitive to censure, the Spider is often distracted or dissuaded by adverse opinions. They should concentrate more on what they are doing and worry less about what others may think. They must also learn to control their desire to overspend. Although their generosity is admirable, extravagance is always a risk. The Spider handles money less well than most, and it may be best to leave financial matters to someone they trust; although those born in this sign are highly talented, monetary and organizational skills are not their forté. Spiders should try to be less self-critical and trust in their abilities, creativity, and intuition; they are often far more capable than they realize.

Suitable Occupations

Writing professions like journalism can be ideal for Spiders, with their inquiring and critical minds. Other suitable professions entail abstract and inventive skills. Being a natural entertainer, acting and the performing arts can be a fitting career for the Spider. Many are also accomplished musicians. Notably, they make excellent lecturers with inventive ways of making their subject matter fascinating. Sales and marketing work can be ideal for the persuasive and imaginative Spider, as can the advertising profession. However, the Spider works best in short, sharp bursts and dislikes being restrained by rules and regulations. Moreover, their rebellious and individualist spirit means that those born in this sign work best alone, and self-employment is an attractive option.

Spiders excel in occupations that employ their analytical skills. They thrive as researchers, scientists, and analysts, where precision is paramount. Their organizational talents make them excellent project managers, but accounting positions are seldom for them. Given their superb memories and entertainment talents, teaching can be a good choice for those born in this sign.

The Spider at Work

Spiders are practical, diligent, and conscientious about their work and are particularly methodical in how they go about it. Walking encyclopedias, their hobbies are often related to their work. The Spider's inability to relax means they frequently take their work home. They have no intention of finishing what they are doing the moment the day ends. Unlike signs that dislike the thought of after-hours work, the Spider usually excels in this way. As colleagues, Spiders are fun to be with, are always willing to help, and are eager to pass on advice. As employers or managers, they can be inspiring and inspirational, motivating and encouraging staff with sheer enthusiasm. As employees, they are hard workers but perform best if they have the freedom to use their creativity. They thrive in organized environments and contribute to maintaining a structured workplace. While they may be perfectionists, their dedication to high standards benefits the entire team. Their friendliness makes them approachable, fostering a collaborative and productive work atmosphere.

The Spider Parent

Those born in this sign make good parents and take a keen interest in their children's education. They raise their young with concern and kindness, are seldom strict, and nearly always refrain from punishment. The Spider treats the child as they would treat an adult, always prepared to explain why something should be done in a particular way. Indeed, Spiders set an excellent example for their children with politeness and considerate manners. Spider parents are attentive, helpful, and observant. They go to great lengths to raise well-behaved and good-mannered children. They want the best for their kids, encouraging them to live a comprehensive lifestyle that includes sports, the arts, and extracurricular pursuits, while ensuring these activities are as enjoyable as possible. Spider parents value education highly and often instill a love of learning in their children. They encourage curiosity and critical thinking, providing ample opportunities for their children to explore and expand their knowledge. They love to spend time helping with homework, engaging in educational activities, and fostering a home environment that supports intellectual growth. They are always there to offer practical advice, lend a helping hand, or provide a listening ear. Their loyalty and dedication create a strong foundation of trust and security.

The Spider Child

Spider children are known for their boundless energy and enthusiasm. They often find it challenging to stay still and are constantly curious and eager to explore and learn. Their vivid imagination helps them make friends easily and occasionally causes conflicts with authority figures due to their strong-willed nature. In an academic setting, Spider children demonstrate great potential, but their restlessness can impede their day-to-day focus. Despite these challenges, their remarkable ability to intensely concentrate allows them to excel in examinations. Spider kids are generally amiable and nonconfrontational. Their natural charisma and quick thinking contribute to their widespread popularity. Additionally, these children display remarkable adaptability from a young age, demonstrating equal enjoyment in solitary play and socializing with others. A child born under the Spider sign displays exceptional curiosity and creativity from an early age. They are natural problem-solvers, often fascinated by puzzles and complex tasks. With a keen eye for detail, they enjoy observing their surroundings and discovering hidden patterns. These children are highly intuitive, quickly picking up on the emotions and intentions of those around them. Their adaptability allows them to thrive in various social situations, and they make friends quickly. Though they can be introspective and enjoy solitary activities, their loyalty and protective instincts ensure they form deep, lasting bonds with family and close friends.

The Spider Friend

Spiders are generous and entertaining friends. Never short of new ideas, they are fun to be around and perhaps the best people to share a night out with. They are also a mine of information, having so many varied interests and experiences that they can keep you engrossed for hours. They are well-mannered and never cause embarrassment unless they intend to. Sometimes, however, Spiders can be a trial. Friends may feel tired or need peace, and along comes the Spider with another great idea. Spiders can't relax. They must keep busy and see that their friends are on the go. Although they have the best intentions, there are times when the Spider will be critical of others, expecting too much, even though they offer constructive advice. They can also be hairsplitters and quibble over minor matters of no consequence. Though loyal to their nearest and dearest, they are clear-sighted about the shortcomings of relatives, partners, and close friends—and sometimes too quick to remind them. Spiders are excellent problem-solvers, bringing their analytical minds to help navigate life's challenges. They offer practical and effective solutions, often assisting friends to see situations from a new perspective. Their honesty and straightforward nature ensure that their advice is genuine and meant for a friend's best interest, even if it comes across as criticism.

The Spider Partner

One of the strangest Spider traits is their failure to realize when they are attractive to a prospective partner. It usually comes as a complete shock when they discover someone is interested in them. This is often considered a lack of interest on the Spider's part—a standard and sometimes sad mistake. The Spider is timid when it comes to starting a relationship, which is due to their self-criticism rather than a lack of confidence.

Although they worry too much and sometimes fail to act, Spiders are generally caring and emotionally uninhibited once they have found the right partner. However, they are usually busy with their careers and are in no hurry to marry or settle down. Moreover, they take great care to get to know someone well before moving in with them. The Spider is usually faithful in a relationship, ensuring one has ended before another begins. They will not forget obligations to an ex-partner, neither will they knowingly be responsible for breaking up someone else's relationship.

Communication with a Spider partner is usually straightforward. They value honesty and transparency and expect the same in return. While they can sometimes be critical, it stems from a desire to improve and strengthen the relationship. They appreciate constructive feedback and are willing to work on their flaws, expecting their partner to be equally committed to personal growth. Those born in this sign are loyal and dependable, providing a solid foundation of trust and security in the relationship. They are not prone to dramatic displays of emotion but express their love through consistent and reliable actions. However, their perfectionist tendencies can sometimes lead to high expectations, which may create pressure for both them and their partner. Balancing their high standards with empathy helps create a more harmonious and supportive partnership. A Spider partner brings dedication, reliability, and thoughtful care, fostering a solid and nurturing relationship.

OROX

★ ★ ★

April 10–May 3

People often look to those born in the cycle of the steady Orox for guidance. They make excellent leaders, and their unwavering determination makes them a beacon of inspiration. Although not lacking imagination, the Orox feels that lofty ideas stand in the way of solid business. They are at their best in difficult situations but may lapse into lethargy if left without a challenge. They are not the best people in the world to initiate a project, but once underway, Orox's leadership qualities offer an invaluable contribution toward success, inspiring and motivating others.

The Orox is the epitome of practicality and common sense. They are seldom impulsive, and their resistance to change is a testament to their stability and reliability. Their firm opinions and convictions make them the most conscientious of all the signs. They have a realistic approach to life, rarely indulging in dreaming or fantasizing. The Orox's grounded nature provides a reassuring and stable presence. Orox individuals are dynamic career people and good socializers, although they often struggle to mix the two. They prefer a well-organized life at work, but they can be somewhat lazy at home. Nevertheless, they need a practical, clean, and uncluttered environment. Oroxes are fond of outdoor life and, if circumstances permit, are enthusiastic gardeners.

The Orox is not one to make large numbers of casual acquaintances; a small circle of close friends is preferred. This preference for quality over quantity in their relationships speaks to the depth of their connections. They are stylish dressers but seldom dress unconventionally, preferring to stick to middle-of-the-road fashion. Uneasy about standing out in a crowd, they refrain from appearing outrageous or unusual. Those born in this sign like to feel secure in their surroundings, so the Orox always looks the part. Although they do not like to stand out because of what they wear or how they behave, the Orox is keen to take a central role in social and sporting activities.

People of this zodiac cycle are always ready to give advice and often the best shoulder to cry on. However, their problems are generally kept hidden, and they are the last to worry others about their concerns. Outwardly, they may seem unemotional; it is difficult to tell what the Orox is thinking or, more importantly, how they feel. Unless angered, Orox people keep their emotions very much to themselves. Nevertheless, this stoicism is often a source of strength, providing a solid foundation for themselves and those around them. The Orox is brave and usually in command of most situations, typically avoiding circumstances where they expect to find trouble. They are confident, consistent, calm, controlled, and effective in most situations. However, the Orox can have a nasty temper if pushed too far.

Those born in this sign undertake most activities precisely and methodically. Being people with regular habits, they are the last to act surprisingly or unexpectedly. Although somewhat predictable, they are good-humored, charismatic, and excellent conversationalists, most having impeccable manners. People born in this sign keep a strict account of their money and economize whenever possible. However, if their income permits, the Orox ensures that the outward trappings are the best they can afford, such as jewelry, a stylish home, and an impressive car. Status symbols are generally crucial for the Orox. Oroxes are hardworking, dependable, and attentive listeners, although they can be somewhat stubborn. People of this zodiac cycle are known for their tireless nature, like a well-built machine that can go on forever. Thanks to their meticulous preparation and planning for every possible scenario, they can overcome most obstacles that come their way.

Sporting activities are high on Orox's list of priorities, and many excel at athletic events. As team players, they make excellent captains.

Those born in this sign excel in sports that require endurance and strength. Their practical nature and patience make them great at long-distance running, cycling, and rowing, where consistent effort is critical. Orox people are also known for their love of nature, often enjoying outdoor sports such as hiking and rock climbing. While they might not be the quickest to start a new sport, their steadfastness ensures they improve steadily and achieve their goals. Team sports benefit from their reliability and a strong sense of loyalty, making them invaluable team players.

Positive Characteristics

The Orox is a symbol of reliability and trustworthiness. They have exceptional leadership powers and a strong will as well as excellent executive skills. With a considerable ability to make money, the Orox is always willing to devote time and effort to the success of an enterprise. Strongly principled, they often possess great courage. With an engaging personality, they usually enjoy robust health and a love of sport, action, and outdoor activities. Those born in this sign can easily judge situations from various perspectives, no matter how challenging. They possess solid observational skills that enable them to comprehend the reasons behind the actions of others. When asked for advice, they offer practical solutions and possess remarkable patience to hear people out. They can work long and hard on projects that require extensive attention for long periods without tiring. The Orox seldom get stressed. They will stop at nothing to succeed when their minds are set. Those of this zodiac cycle have a down-to-earth attitude and a calm demeanor that puts associates and loved ones at ease. Excellent multitaskers, Oroxes pay close attention to detail, cope well with difficulties, and adapt quickly to overcome obstacles. They often assume principal roles in political or social groups where leadership qualities are highly valued.

Negative Characteristics

An overbearing attitude may reduce the chances of social success, while a headstrong temperament matched by intolerance can lead to conflict. Errors of judgment are sometimes made due to strongly biased opinions. Many born in this sign share unrealistic expectations of others, and stubborn adherence to ideas can make relationships difficult. Sometimes, the Orox can be arrogant, conceited, and egotistic. They take a firm stand and generally refuse to budge. They tend to procrastinate and dwell on matters for too long before arriving at a decision. The Orox usually only likes to engage in events they initiate, and it is hard to convince them to join in with activities arranged by others. They can expect too much from friends, loved ones, and colleagues. Sometimes, the Orox can be controlling and possessive. Although tidy, they are often hoarders, refusing to dispose of belongings they no longer use or those that are broken beyond repair. They can be possessive and overly materialistic, overvaluing possessions and comfort. Oroxes may also be slow to forgive and hold grudges, finding it difficult to relinquish past grievances. Their practicality can sometimes come off as a lack of imagination or spontaneity. Additionally, they may struggle with being overly cautious and hesitant to take risks or embrace new ideas.

Appearance

Those born in this sign are often sturdy in appearance, have firm features, and share a confident and authoritative stature. The Orox usually looks you straight in the eyes while exuding a commanding presence. They often have large eyes and prominent eyebrows and tend to possess a defined facial bone structure. Although Orox is a sign of activity, it is not a sign of nervous energy; therefore, there may be a tendency toward being overweight, particularly after middle age. They have a calm and collected demeanor and are generally relaxed—at least in outward appearance. They are usually charming and comfortable in company, even amongst strangers, exuding confidence and control.

Health

Throat infections are common for those born during this sign, especially in childhood, where frequent bouts of tonsillitis are common. As this is a physically active sign, injuries and broken limbs are frequent. Some people may be slim or skinny, no matter their lifestyle, but generally, the Orox must make a concerted effort regarding diet or exercise to remain in good shape. Many born in this sign are susceptible to colds, bronchitis, and other respiratory infections. They tend to have good eyesight, but hearing may be problematic later in life. Oroxes often have robust health and a strong constitution, benefiting from their practical approach to life and appreciation for routine. They thrive on stability, making them more likely to adopt consistent health practices. However, their love for indulgence can sometimes lead to overeating and a sedentary lifestyle.

The Formula for Success

The Orox is an exceptionally patient sign, and most apply themselves with continued diligence to any enterprise. In business matters, they make excellent spokespeople, able to negotiate the best bargains. The Orox, however, is not the ideal sign for initiating a new project, being suspicious of the risks involved. Experimentation is not an Orox trait; most born in this sign are reluctant gamblers. They prefer to keep their feet firmly on the ground and have excellent administrative ability. The Orox is usually the most suitable manager in business affairs and leader in sporting activities. They are capable organizers and keep a firm grip on financial matters. Moreover, they are always ready to assume command and are unafraid to exercise authority or make important decisions. Oroxes are highly reliable, often becoming the backbone of recreational and professional settings. Their patience allows them to navigate challenges steadily, and their appreciation for quality usually leads to excellence in their endeavors. Additionally, their strong sense of loyalty fosters long-lasting relationships.

Words of Advice

Those born in this sign are often overcautious and share a stubborn reluctance to take chances. They may be highly competent organizers and administrators, but experimentation and risk-taking are best left to others. Sometimes, their hesitance can be a handicap; frequently, they fail to explore their capabilities or realize their full potential. They often become set in their ways, finding it difficult to adapt to new situations. For the best results, the Orox should learn to take the occasional risk and realize that failures are often an essential part of learning. The Orox is inclined to be thrifty, although they like to be seen as successful, so an inclination to acquire status symbols, such as flashy cars or expensive designer clothes, can be a trend for those born in this sign. They will benefit significantly by having a friend, manager, or partner who can offer sound counseling on such areas of extravagance. Oroxes should embrace their natural determination and patience and use their strong work ethic to achieve their goals. However, they must remember to balance hard work with relaxation. The Orox should trust their instincts and stay true to their values; reliability is one of their greatest assets. Nevertheless, they should be open to change and new experiences, even if these challenge their comfort zone.

Suitable Occupations

Oroxes prefer occupations that offer steady advancement and long-term security. Their enviable patience sees them through times of difficulty, usually leading to supervisory or managerial roles in their chosen line of work. Those born in this cycle are good with money, so financial careers have considerable appeal. They make excellent bankers, although work involving financial speculation is not the forté of the cautious Orox. They are usually successful in whatever occupation they choose. They make sensible and responsible decisions in management and are conscientious workers. This is a versatile sign regarding employment, and most born in this cycle can learn almost any trade. Oroxes are practical, reliable, and have a strong work ethic. These traits make them well suited for various occupations that value stability, attention to detail, and a steady, hands-on approach. They often excel in finance-related careers, such as accounting and fiscal planning. Their methodical nature and ability to work with numbers ensure they accurately manage monetary matters. Practical and reliable, Oroxes can succeed as architects, civil engineers, or construction managers.

The Orox at Work

The Orox is a sign of fixed character. If a change in outlook or direction is required in their working environment, the Orox may find adjusting hard. They are consistent in outlook, habits, and behavior and pursue a professional objective with continued application and dedication. They make the most steadfast of colleagues, and fellow workers generally know exactly where they stand with the Orox. As employers, individuals with this sign are especially aware of the needs and abilities of those for whom they are responsible. However, they expect others to commit to an enterprise with as much dedication as themselves. The Orox is a diligent employee, although they do not necessarily mix well with their colleagues. They are easy enough to get along with during working hours, but the Orox usually draws a strict dividing line between work and social life. Often, their friends are from an entirely separate circle of acquaintances.

The Orox Parent

Home life is essential to the Orox, and family roots run deep. They are one of the most caring signs when it comes to the well-being of their children, although emotionally, they may be somewhat reserved. They encourage their young in schoolwork but may be unresponsive to social and personal problems. Typically, they feel that others will be as strong as they are and tend to lack sympathy with those in emotional crises. Putting a problem to the back of the mind may be easy for the Orox, but others are not so strong. Those born in this sign always ensure that their children are well-dressed, fed, and cared for, no matter what personal sacrifices are necessary. Orox parents can provide a strong foundation for their children's lives, offering practical and patient encouragement. They rarely get angry, annoyed, or irritated when a child makes mistakes or takes time to learn. The Orox is often keen on health and fitness and is into eating healthy foods—a positive influence on their child's well-being. They can create a stable and caring home. However, those born in this sign may be overprotective and take time to accept when their offspring are ready to live a life of their own.

The Orox Child

The Orox child is a responsive and eager learner from an early age. They are curious, wanting to know the whole reason for everything. They are seldom put off with a half-answer. They work diligently at school and usually do well in class. There are rarely bad reports of the Orox child. They are keen to succeed in sports, and many become school captains. Those of this zodiac cycle prefer routine and dislike environmental change. A new school or home move can easily upset the young Orox, although conversely, they are generally content and easy to please if their surroundings remain consistent. The Orox has a constructive attitude to life, and few Orox children will deliberately cause trouble or break their toys. They are exceptionally polite to adults, but there is a tendency for the Orox child to be overbearing with other children. The Orox is not afraid of hard work and is willing to do whatever it takes to get the job done. Kids doing class projects are fortunate to have an Orox in their group or team. In addition to their hardworking nature, they possess a high level of ambition and mental tenacity, making them a force to be reckoned with.

The Orox Friend

The Orox is peace-loving and amiable, wishing to live harmoniously with their associates and neighbors. Few are responsible for causing trouble of any kind. When annoyed, however, they have quite a temper. Beware of trying the patience of the Orox. Once hurt or angered, the Orox is slow to forgive and will seldom forget. They make loyal and supportive friends, but others should avoid crossing them. They can be possessive in relationships and friendships alike. They choose their acquaintances carefully, ensuring they mix with others who share their beliefs and sentiments. Accordingly, there are seldom conflicts of interest. However, if one of their friends should change their attitudes or find others with whom to associate, the Orox may feel personally snubbed. Those born in this sign make devoted friends but are uneasy about casual acquaintances. Although competitive, they take defeat well and behave with grace when beaten.

The Orox Partner

The Orox is an uninhibited lover, although romantic sentiment is not a natural trait. Many marry young to establish order and routine, sometimes leading to hasty decisions and affiliations. Marriage can be one of the only times in the Orox's life when they do not think long and hard about a commitment. The Orox will ensure a partnership succeeds if the right partner is found. They are usually the most loyal partners of any sign. Those born in this cycle are especially hurt when a relationship fails. Breakups demoralize the Orox considerably, and their entire life may suffer. When a relationship ends, the Orox sees it as a personal failure. They have considerable difficulty coping with turmoil or coming to terms with change. The Orox values stability and predictability. They thrive in relationships with a clear sense of security and routine. This preference for consistency means that an Orox lover is less likely to engage in drama or emotional turbulence. Instead, they provide a calming, reassuring presence, which can be comforting for partners who crave a sense of safety and reliability.

An Orox partner is loyal, dependable, and known for unwavering support. They value stability and consistency in relationships, making them reliable and devoted companions. They are generally affectionate and enjoy creating a comfortable and harmonious home environment. They appreciate the finer things in life and often express their love through thoughtful gestures and quality time. However, they can be stubborn and resistant to change, preferring routine and familiarity. This stubbornness is a double-edged sword; while it can create challenges, it also means that Oroxes are steadfast and unlikely to give up on their relationship quickly. Their patience, sensuality, and commitment create a robust and enduring bond in a partnership, making them ideal for those seeking a long-term, steady relationship. They will invest time and effort into building an enduring bond. This patience, combined with their sensual nature, makes them attentive lovers who prioritize their partner's needs and desires.

MOUFLON

☆ ☆ ☆

May 4–May 21

In Mesopotamian tradition, these wild sheep were considered helpful spirit animals. Acting as intermediaries between Heaven and Earth, they were thought to influence dreams and imagination. Like their mythical counterparts, those born in the Mouflon cycle are creative, intuitive, and imaginative. As natural actors and charmers, they are never more in their element than in the public eye. Spirit mouflons of legend could inspire foresight; they had the power to influence the future and bring magic and mystery into the world. Accordingly, mystical subjects often appeal strongly to those born in this sign, and there is a marked tendency for Mouflons to hold unusual or revolutionary ideas. The Mouflon is born with a romantic and alluring personality, a love of adventure, and a passion for romance. They are often dreamers, so their true intentions can be hard to fathom.

Mouflons are known for their love of variety and adventure, although they are not as daring as some signs. They value their comfort and security too much to risk them in all-or-nothing endeavors. The celestial mouflon of legend journeyed from the gods to humanity and is reflected in this sign's strong desire to travel. However, Mouflons are hesitant to leave the place they call home. They need a secure environment to return to. While generally kind and helpful, they have strong preferences and little patience for those they don't connect with. It's usually clear whether a Mouflon likes or dislikes someone.

Many Mouflons exude a timeless aura of youth. There is something of the child in those born in this sign; few outgrow the desire for fun, frolics, and frivolity. Consequently, they are not the most eager of signs to settle down and raise a family. Mouflons enjoy adventure and romance far too much to throw it all away at the first opportunity. After much deliberation, they ultimately choose a partner to share their lives with. People born in this sign can appear open and friendly in social situations but prefer to play it cool, giving little away about themselves. They dislike parties and pre-planned social events, preferring a more spontaneous form of socializing. Although generally good-humored, the Mouflon is not beyond resorting to conflict if necessary and has a temper if pushed too far. They can be somewhat possessive and typically refuse to give up old ideas and obsolete belongings, which can result in them being something of a hoarder. Their good humor often lightens the mood, making them a joy.

The Mouflon takes great pride in their appearance and is often keen on physical fitness, healthy living, and strenuous recreational activities, devoting much time to keeping in shape. They have a fondness for athletics and sport. Even if they are not personally involved in the competition, they will be keen to follow their favorite team or competitors. The Mouflon is an ardent supporter and an enthusiastic spectator. They love a challenge, provided it does not disrupt their lifestyle. They intend to enjoy every moment. Most Mouflons are fun-loving. However, beyond the contented veneer of the Mouflon lies a powerful drive to succeed and a spirit of pure determination.

Mouflons are known for their enigmatic nature and independence, making them a mystery. Despite their keenness to socialize, they tend to keep their personal lives guarded, making them complex to figure out and difficult to get to know. Those born in this zodiac cycle seldom doubt or lack confidence and can often be vain. They have a wealth of charm and appeal and can be exceptionally charismatic. Mouflons are passionate and usually approach life with fierce determination. They are unafraid of challenges and have a unique ability to rise after defeat. This resilience and resourcefulness make them adept at navigating life's complexities, and they emerge stronger from adversity. Mouflons possess a natural magnetism that can draw people in, often creating an aura of mystery around them. Their penetrating gaze and keen observational skills allow them to profoundly understand people and situations, frequently seeing beyond the surface.

Positive Characteristics

Big ideas and ambitions are complemented by lively intelligence. There is a love of travel and adventure, and artistic pursuits have a strong appeal. Often popular, a Mouflon's enthusiasm can bring out the best in others. They can be fascinating and are quick with compliments. Many born in this sign have talents connected with the performing arts. They have keen powers of observation and are quick to grasp the essence of most situations. With an appealing imagination and an intense appreciation of beauty, many Mouflons share an interest in environmental issues. Mouflons are known for their self-belief and confidence and are not easily intimidated. Those born in this sign are unpredictable and never dull. When a Mouflon sets their mind on something, they pursue it with unwavering focus and determination, making it difficult to deter them from achieving their goals. Mouflons are also known for their strategic thinking and problem-solving abilities. They approach challenges meticulously and calculatedly, often creating innovative solutions. Their determination and focus enable them to achieve their goals, no matter how difficult or ambitious. Despite being highly active, Mouflon individuals have a gentle and compassionate side, making them excellent friends and partners. Their empathetic and nurturing qualities allow them to connect deeply with others, offering support and understanding. Their innate kindness and generosity inspire those around them, fostering a sense of community and mutual respect.

Negative Characteristics

Mouflons have difficulty concentrating, especially when they have too much on their minds. Few find it easy to handle more than one problem at a time. Failure to apply themselves to intricate endeavors may reduce their chances of success. Worry and indecision also hold back progress for many born in this sign. Mouflons hate to feel they are being manipulated, and often, resentment of authority can complicate relationships in business or the workplace. Many Mouflons are dreamers and share unrealistic expectations concerning their activities. They do not recover quickly from failure; stagnation may result from an unsuccessful enterprise. They can be vain and arrogant and refuse to admit mistakes even when they know they are in the wrong. Most Mouflons will rely on others to tidy up after them, almost as if they believe they were not put on this Earth to perform menial tasks. Although it can be a great strength, a particular problem for the Mouflon is that they don't know when to give up. Intensity can manifest as possessiveness and jealousy for those born in this sign, making them overly controlling in relationships. They are often secretive, guarding their emotions and thoughts closely, which can lead to misunderstandings and a perceived lack of trustworthiness. Additionally, their strong desire for control and power can make them manipulative and domineering, creating conflicts in their personal and professional lives. While known for their dynamic and energetic nature, Mouflon individuals can exhibit several negative characteristics. Their strong drive and ambition can sometimes translate into impatience and a short temper, making them prone to frustration when things don't go their way. The Mouflon's impulsive nature may lead to hasty decisions without fully considering the consequences. Their desire to lead and be in control can come across as bossy or overly aggressive, potentially alienating others. Additionally, they can be self-centered, focusing more on their goals and desires rather than considering the needs and feelings of those around them.

Appearance

Those born in this sign are usually graceful and elegant and move with a purposeful and determined gait. Most Mouflon activities are conducted with deliberate and mindful composure. They refuse to sprawl or slouch even when relaxed. Few Mouflons will be scruffy or unkempt in any circumstance. They do, however, share a lazy attitude concerning laborious domestic chores. Mouflons have significant, expressive facial features and move more slowly than some signs. They often possess robust, well-defined bone structures, prominent cheekbones, and a firm gaze. The Mouflon has a captivating appearance and a determined look. They usually dress well and move with confidence. Mouflons often have a striking and magnetic physical appearance that reflects their intense and enigmatic nature. They typically possess piercing eyes that seem to look straight into the soul, a feature many find captivating. Their aura is mysterious and alluring, drawing others in with an almost hypnotic charm.

Health

Individuals born in this cycle typically possess a robust immune system, allowing for good overall health and swift recovery. Few Mouflons will suffer bouts of colds or flu. Indeed, viral infections are rare for Mouflons after childhood. Allergies are the most common complaints of this group. The Mouflon's highly active immune system can often result in problems such as allergies, asthma, or hay fever. Many Mouflons suffer skin rashes caused by an adverse reaction to dust, fur, and certain foods. Problems with the knees and lower back are common. Mouflons may be prone to certain health issues due to their intense nature and emotional depth. Stress and anxiety can manifest physically, leading to problems such as headaches, ulcers, and high blood pressure. Their tendency to internalize emotions might contribute to digestive issues. Additionally, their predisposition to intense emotions can make them susceptible to mental health challenges, such as depression and mood swings.

The Formula for Success

Mouflons are generous and kind to their relatives and loved ones. They are particularly receptive to the problems of those close to them; always ready to listen, they provide a firm shoulder to cry on. They are highly ambitious, although they may need the support and direction of others to fulfill their dreams. However, this is seldom a problem as the Mouflon is one of the most influential signs; they have the enviable ability to affect the attitudes and decisions of others. Those born in this cycle possess extraordinary intuition, enabling them to predict or determine the actions and intentions of those around them. Their hunches and insights often prove uncannily accurate in various walks of life. Mouflons are known for their determination, one of their most prominent traits. Once they have decided on something, they will pursue it with great focus and won't hold back. Little can deter a Mouflon from achieving their goals.

Words of Advice

Mouflons are expressive but have difficulty articulating heartfelt emotions. If their love and affection are not reciprocated, they may become withdrawn. They do not respond well to failures in business and friendships or rejection in love. The Mouflon is also inconsistent in temperament and is inclined to be silent or moody at times. Those born in this sign are strongly advised not to expect too much from others or from what may seem a promising endeavor. The Mouflon is also one of the worst signs for timekeeping and always leaves things to the last possible moment. Those born in this sign need plenty of time to prepare and are often late. Imaginative temperament results in absent-mindedness. Moreover, they tend to daydream. Mouflons will lapse into reverie if they are engaged in something that fails to absorb their attention entirely. Most of all, Mouflons are forgetful and forever mislaying their possessions. The Mouflon should learn to concentrate. More significantly, they should avoid putting off until later what can quickly be done immediately. Those born in this sign should practice forgiveness, even when challenging. They should trust in their resilience during tough times and not shy away from seeking help.

Suitable Occupations

The Mouflon is a paradoxical sign regarding work. They have lofty and far-reaching ambitions but need the constant support and encouragement of others. If without a cause, a lack of self-motivation may lead Mouflons to drift into occupations they cannot abide. Ideally, however, anything connected with entertainment is the perfect career for those born into this sign. Drama has strong appeal, as does singing and music. The Mouflon has excellent coordination, and many Mouflons make superb dancers. Careers in the travel or leisure industry are also appealing to Mouflons. Having a flair for the dramatic, Mouflons make good publicists. Individuals born under the Mouflon zodiac sign are often well suited for careers in finance and investment due to their determination and resourcefulness. They possess the ability to analyze and assess risks; coupled with their strong desire to achieve their goals, they are likely to excel in roles such as analysts, stockbrokers, or investment consultants.

The Mouflon at Work

The Mouflon has strong likes and dislikes. Few born in this sign will spare much time for those they disapprove of. This may lead to complications in working relationships. Mouflons find it challenging and tiresome to exchange niceties or feign affinity with colleagues or business acquaintances to achieve results, and this honest and forthright manner can often prejudice success or career advancement. The Mouflon may be an enthusiastic and dedicated boss but will likely favor some employees over others. This can be detrimental to the smooth running of a business, and resignations are common when an enterprise appoints a new Mouflon manager. However, before long, the Mouflon will gather around them the team with whom they are happiest to work. They make few pretensions with opponents. Most people who fall on the wrong side of a Mouflon are unlikely to remain around for long. Nevertheless, if Mouflons can check their emotions, their ability to stay focused and dedicated makes them excellent leaders and reliable team members.

The Mouflon Parent

Most Mouflons share the need to live in a clean, uncluttered environment. Unfortunately, they hate the mundane work of keeping their homes neat. The desire for order usually outweighs their lazy streak;

housework and other domestic chores will eventually be done. Once they have undertaken the considerable effort necessary to complete these laborious tasks, they will not take kindly to someone coming along and messing things up. A prime trait of Mouflon parents is to go to great lengths to keep their children from being dirty or untidy. They allow specific rooms as playrooms, ruling other parts of the house out of bounds. They can be strict with their children regarding personal appearance, although Mouflons can be lenient in other matters. They are liberal in outlook, seldom expecting their offspring to share their views. Few Mouflons try to force an unwanted career upon their children and tend to support whatever their young ones eventually decide to do.

The Mouflon Child

Mouflon children have solid attachments and deep bonds with their parents. Provided they are raised in a happy home, few born in this sign will be eager to leave. The Mouflon child is ultra-sensitive to the family atmosphere and is quick to respond to the moods of parents or siblings. It is essential that their environment should be calm and happy. Mouflon children are especially susceptible to the negative influence of parental quarrels, even in adolescence. They are honest and loving children, although overconfidence and a stubborn streak can lead to problems with adults, teachers, and those in authority. Mouflons tend to be astute and streetwise at a young age and are usually leaders among their friends.

The Mouflon Friend

The Mouflon is a friendly sign, although most born in this cycle refuse to indulge in idle gossip. Accordingly, they make trustworthy friends. Acquaintances can rest assured that their secrets are safe with those born in this cycle. Something told to them in confidence is unlikely to be shared with others. Indeed, this is the least meddlesome of any sign. For the Mouflon, other people's business is their private affair. Due to their fine intuition, Mouflons have a mysterious, ethereal quality. So often, they know exactly what someone is thinking and take the relevant action at the right time. Listening carefully and considering their ideas and proposals is a word of advice for their friends and acquaintances. Their insights are frequently well-founded, and their hunches are often accurate. They are, however, inclined to change their plans at the last moment. Although romantic, the Mouflon is not the best person for remembering birthdays, anniversaries, and special occasions. If they have forgotten a significant engagement, friends should avoid taking offense or thinking that this is in any way a personal rebuff. Mouflons can even forget their own birthdays. Those born in this sign share idealistic attitudes to relationships and can expect too much from friends. It is best to let the Mouflon know precisely what they can expect from you, which they will generally accept and act accordingly.

The Mouflon Partner

Although at ease in the limelight, the Mouflon needs personal space. This is particularly true for their privacy of mind. One thing that Mouflons cannot stand is someone asking them what they are thinking or what is going through their mind. Partners should not be tempted to ask why the Mouflon seems remote or lost in a world of thought. They are likely to be told to mind their own business. Time to think alone is an essential requirement in the life of any Mouflon. Their partners should remember this: the Mouflon may love them dearly, but encroachment on their personal space is certainly not appreciated. Despite their tough exteriors, Mouflons are sensitive and protective of their loved ones. They might not always express their feelings openly, but their actions speak volumes. Understanding a Mouflon's need for privacy and occasional solitude is crucial; it allows them to process their emotions and recharge.

The Mouflon is far less impulsive than many signs in their attitude to love and marriage. Even when deeply attracted to someone, it will be some time before they can make any firm commitments. The whole relationship may be dissolved if dating is not allowed to proceed slowly, carefully, stage by stage. Rush the Mouflon, and you may risk everything. Indeed, Mouflons hate to be hurried at anything in their lives. Few Mouflons are prepared to abandon their former lives for the sake of anyone, even their partner. Nevertheless, Mouflons are generous, warmhearted, and loyal, although sometimes possessive, even, and jealous. Communication is vital in mitigating these tendencies. Those born in this sign can be suspicious of something in which they are kept in the dark.

VULTURE

☆ ☆ ☆

May 22–June 10

In Mesopotamian mythology, the vulture symbolized prowess, adventure, tactics, strategy, and foresight. Individuals born under this sign share an adventurous spirit coupled with thought and preplanning. They may be courageous, but they are careful. Vultures are practical and intuitive, with exceptional skills to address situations from an overall perspective. They also have the enviable ability to empathize and appreciate the viewpoints of others. People born during this sign often have captivating and attentive personalities within a calm and composed exterior. They are driven by a strong sense of purpose and possess an innate understanding of fairness and morality. One of the Vulture's advantageous qualities is their readiness to acknowledge and rectify their mistakes. They are unafraid to adapt their opinions and approaches, showing a genuine willingness to grow and evolve. They value constructive criticism as essential to personal development and frequently seek input from their friends and peers.

Vultures are often the visionaries of the zodiac. Their minds are always buzzing with new ideas and concepts driven by a natural curiosity about the world around them. This intellectual curiosity leads them to explore various fields, from science and technology to philosophy and social issues. They thrive on understanding complex systems and are adept at thinking outside the box. This makes them excellent problem-solvers, capable of devising innovative solutions that others might overlook. Their inventive nature is not just limited to their professional lives; it permeates all aspects of their existence, making them fascinating conversationalists and insightful friends.

Vultures are highly adaptable. They are not afraid of change; they often seek it out. They understand that growth and progress usually require stepping out of one's comfort zone and embracing the unknown. This adaptability allows them to navigate life's ups and downs with grace and resilience. They are forward-thinking and continually seek ways to improve and evolve personally and collectively. Like all signs, Vultures have their challenges. Their strong need for independence can sometimes lead to isolation or difficulty forming close relationships. Their preference for logic over emotion can make them appear detached or unempathetic. However, these challenges also present growth opportunities. By learning to balance their intellectual pursuits with emotional awareness and finding ways to connect with others on a deeper level, Vultures can enhance their relationships and overall well-being.

Vultures possess exceptional skills in assessing situations impartially. They generally avoid taking sides during conflicts and approach situations with a fair and unbiased perspective. These admirable qualities enable Vultures to develop comprehensive plans and make rational decisions. Before acting, Vultures carefully observe, listen, and absorb information, demonstrating a thoughtful and deliberate approach to conflict resolution. Despite their personal beliefs, Vultures strive to acknowledge and appreciate the validity of all viewpoints, indicating their open-mindedness and willingness to consider different perspectives. Additionally, Vultures are receptive to persuasion, especially when presented with solid reasoning and hard evidence.

Individuals born under the sign of Vulture are socially adaptable and excel in intellectual conversations. They are deeply committed to their unconventional beliefs and can transition from enthusiastic conversationalists to contemplative thinkers in moments. Despite forming meaningful connections, they may come across as distant at times. It's essential for those who know the Vulture to embrace and appreciate them for who they are. Mental privacy is paramount to the Vulture, who will passionately defend it. They may have, in an unorthodox manner, inscrutable and complex motives. By contrast, those born in this sign are fascinated by the intentions and motivations of others. Be they friends, lovers, or mere acquaintances, Vultures are determined to discover just what it is that makes people tick. Therefore, those born in this sign have a paradoxical, enigmatic personality that others can find enchanting.

Positive Characteristics

Vultures are known for their energetic, engaging, and vibrant personalities. They often find themselves in the spotlight due to their dramatic flair and flamboyant nature and exude confidence in most situations. Their unique ability to see the bigger picture, mystical inclination, and well-developed intuition draw many of them to philosophical and spiritual pursuits. With their creativity, adaptability, and imagination, Vultures are often seen as original thinkers with distinctive ideas. Their sense of humor greatly contributes to their social success. Driven by their ambition, Vultures continually set and achieve admirable goals through hard work, determination, and concerted effort. Their constant drive to outperform themselves and others motivates them to overcome difficulties. These qualities ensure that many individuals born under this sign succeed in their professional and leisure endeavors. Whether it's excelling as exceptional athletes or dominating in the world of online gaming, Vultures thrive with a competitive spirit and determination. Vultures possess a natural curiosity and a keen intellect, often thinking outside the box to find unique solutions. Independence and originality are their hallmarks, making them trailblazers in their fields. They are highly social and valued community members, often engaging in humanitarian efforts to improve the world. Their forward-thinking nature makes them visionaries, always looking ahead to new possibilities. Vultures are also known for their friendliness and open-mindedness, embracing diversity and encouraging others to express their true selves. Their optimism and creativity inspire those around them.

❋ Negative Characteristics

Those born during the sign of the Vulture display a remarkable ability to immerse themselves in intricate mental landscapes, often escaping into their imagination when confronted with obstacles. Although their vivid inner world allows them to dream big, this tendency can sometimes hinder their success in practical matters, leading to dashed hopes from unrealistic expectations. This inclination toward wishful thinking also poses potential risks in business endeavors. The Vulture's outspoken nature and unconventional perspectives may attract criticism, as they are not afraid to express their opinions. While they excel at managing their households with practicality and skill, their disinterest in financial matters can lead to personal challenges. Vultures throw themselves wholeheartedly into their endeavors, often becoming intensely focused and overly enthusiastic, sometimes to the exclusion of friends, family, and partners. Their pursuit of perfectionism means they view failure as a considerable setback rather than a challenge to conquer or move beyond. When faced with setbacks, their resulting despondency can have a ripple effect on the emotions of those around them. Their strong desire for independence sometimes makes Vultures appear aloof or detached, leading to difficulties forming deep emotional connections. Their focus on innovation and unconventional ideas might come across as stubbornness or an unwillingness to conform. They can be unpredictable, often changing their plans or interests abruptly. Additionally, their tendency to prioritize intellectual pursuits over emotions can make them seem distant or unempathetic. While their forward-thinking nature is admirable, it can sometimes lead to impracticality or a lack of attention to more immediate details and responsibilities.

❋ Appearance

People born during the sign of Vulture often have expressive and intense eyes that reveal their thoughtful and determined nature. Many possess a striking combination of tall foreheads and distinct widow's peaks, which adds to their commanding presence. Despite their quick reflexes, they move with deliberate and purposeful strides, giving off an air of calculated intention with every step. Even in moments of relaxation, it's rare to see individuals born under this sign slouching or sprawled out, maintaining a poised and upright posture. Their naturally slender builds and distinct facial features contribute to their unwavering and authoritative demeanor. From their deep and resolute gazes to prominent cheekbones and defined browbones, individuals born under this sign exude a sense of determination and strength.

Health

Vulture individuals are known for their remarkable dedication and perseverance in pursuing their goals and aspirations. This steadfast commitment may sometimes lead to feelings of stress and anxiety. Still, they excel in managing their lives to minimize the likelihood of experiencing digestive or stomach-related issues. Vultures exhibit extraordinary resilience, with bodies that possess an incredible ability for rapid healing and recovery from injuries. Broken bones have a remarkable propensity for swift healing, and any cuts or bruises tend to heal and fade in a relatively short period of time.

The Formula for Success

Vultures are known for their strong moral compass and commitment to truth, sincerity, and idealism. Their decision-making is a blend of logical reasoning and intuitive insight, which positions them well for success in various pursuits. They are renowned for their industrious nature, keen intellect, and adeptness at communicating clearly and persuasively. In social settings, they are affable, easygoing with acquaintances, undemanding as friends, and supportive as colleagues. Vultures possess a remarkable capacity for imaginative thinking and a rare ability to empathize and understand diverse perspectives. Few Vultures rush to judgment; they meticulously analyze all facets of a problem before arriving at conclusions, often producing innovative and revolutionary ideas. Known for their unparalleled creativity and a treasury of original concepts, Vultures also boast exceptional flexibility, a vibrant imagination, and a remarkable sense of humor that enriches their social interactions. They are marked by unyielding ambition and a propensity for setting and attaining commendable goals through unwavering determination.

Words of Advice

Vultures tend to be idealists, often finding solace in daydreams and even fantasies when faced with daunting challenges. This inclination toward escapism can lead them to become introverted, secretive, and emotionally distant as they seek to evade the harsh realities of life. Vultures must acknowledge and confront these tendencies, understanding that life does not always unfold as expected. They assume they are immune to failure because they are usually good at anticipating problems and planning well. Additionally, Vultures may find themselves engrossed in their work to excess. When they believe in a cause, they wholeheartedly dedicate themselves to it, sometimes at the cost of relationships, family life, and daily responsibilities. Recognizing and addressing this deeply committed yet potentially obsessive aspect of their character is vital for the well-being of Vultures.

Suitable Occupations

Individuals born under the sign of Vulture often possess a natural inclination toward seeking the spotlight and demonstrate exceptional skills in public speaking, performing arts, and endeavors requiring the art of persuasion. Many accomplished advertising professionals and executives are born under this sign. They are adept at leveraging their innate charm and proficient communication skills to achieve success in their careers. Moreover, the Vulture's practical and analytical inclinations make them well suited for roles in engineering and technology, enabling them to effectively utilize their problem-solving capabilities and innovative mindset to develop and improve complex systems and products. Their unwavering dedication and ability to focus also make them well-equipped for careers in computer science and information technology, as they excel in tasks that demand precision and meticulous attention to detail. Those born under this astrological sign possess an unquenchable thirst for knowledge, which drives some to pursue academic interests and expand their understanding of the world. Their bold and inquisitive nature makes them well suited for scientific research, where they can challenge existing boundaries and contribute to humanity's collective knowledge.

The Vulture at Work

Individuals born under the Vulture sign are known for their remarkable ability to adapt to various work situations and flexibility in handling tasks. They possess a deep understanding of people and are known for their empathetic nature, making them exceptionally well suited for leadership roles. A Vulture employer embodies traits such as a strong sense of fairness, an unwavering work ethic, and the ability to set a positive example for others. Additionally, Vulture employees excel in fostering positive and harmonious relationships with their peers. They have a natural talent for mediating conflicts and resolving issues with fairness and justice. For Vultures, the ideal profession involves challenges and opportunities to take on leadership roles. They thrive in environments that provide stimulation and avenues for creative expression. Without these elements, they are unlikely to find lasting contentment in their work. Vultures are innovative, forward-thinking, and excellent problem-solvers in the workplace. They bring creativity and fresh ideas to any team, often challenging conventional methods and proposing unique solutions. Their intellectual curiosity drives them to continuously learn and improve, making them valuable assets in dynamic environments. They work well in collaborative settings, valuing teamwork and diverse perspectives. However, their independent nature also means they excel in roles that allow for autonomy and creative freedom. Vulture employees are dedicated to their work and often champion causes or projects that align with their humanitarian values, striving to make a positive impact.

The Vulture Parent

As parents, Vultures are devoted to developing their children's critical thinking skills and self-sufficiency. They excel at incorporating innovation and passion into everyday academic subjects, making learning enriching and enjoyable. Unlike some parents, Vultures refrain from imposing their interests and beliefs on their children, encouraging them to explore and develop their identities. Moreover, Vulture parents prioritize actively listening to their children, approaching their concerns with an open mind and without bias before making judgments. Those born under this astrological sign are known for their unwavering commitment to hard work and relentless determination to provide their families with a secure and comfortable life. They stress the importance of instilling values such as responsibility, dedication, and pragmatism in their children. Vulture parents endeavor to create a nurturing and supportive environment where their children can thrive and feel safe.

The Vulture Child

Children born under the influence of the Vulture cycle share extraordinary levels of creativity and determination. They relentlessly pursue their goals and demonstrate keen intellect and exceptional intuition. As a result, they often take on significant responsibilities early in life. Their insatiable curiosity about the world around them drives them to seek knowledge, constantly satisfying their inquisitive nature. However, their intense curiosity may make it challenging to focus during school, as they can quickly become lost in daydreams or captivated by external stimuli. Nonetheless, when they do concentrate, their exceptional creativity shines through, leading to remarkable achievements. Although they are physically capable of excelling in sports, Vulture children prioritize solitary activities over group or organized events.

The Vulture Friend

A Vulture friend is a valuable addition to anyone's life, bringing creativity, intellect, and genuine care for those around them. Known for their innovative and forward-thinking nature, they approach friendship with an open mind and a readiness to embrace new experiences. They are often the ones to introduce fresh ideas and activities, making the friendship dynamic and evolving. One of the most notable traits of a Vulture friend is their deep sense of individuality. They value their freedom and encourage their friends to do the same. This respect for individuality fosters a nonjudgmental environment where everyone feels comfortable being their true selves. The Vulture champions diversity and inclusivity, welcoming people from all walks of life into their circle. Intellectual stimulation is a cornerstone of their friendships. They enjoy deep conversations about various topics, from philosophy and science to social issues and the arts. Their curiosity and thirst for knowledge make them excellent conversationalists who can inspire and challenge their friends to think differently.

The Vulture Partner

Vultures have high expectations of their partners, which can be challenging. This can lead to disappointment, but Vultures usually try to find a balanced relationship approach. Once committed, Vultures are known for their loyalty and intense emotional investment as partners, although they prefer to keep public displays of affection to a minimum. Vultures believe successful relationships are possible if their partners respect their desire for independence and personal freedom. Vultures strongly dislike any intrusion in their lives, regardless of the well-meaning intentions behind it. They may also need to take a temporary hiatus from the world and seek solitude for introspection and contemplation. During these periods, they often withdraw from social interactions. It's crucial for partners to understand that this need for solitude does not reflect their relationship and to recognize that Vultures simply require space to process their thoughts.

With the necessary space, Vultures will soon emerge from their contemplative state.

The Vulture's creativity and originality make them fascinating partners who are always full of surprises. They thrive on deep, meaningful conversations and enjoy discussing numerous topics. This intellectual connection is crucial for them as they seek a partner who can challenge and inspire them mentally. Emotionally, those born in this sign may appear aloof or detached. However, they are deeply caring and loyal once they commit. They express their love through actions rather than overt displays of affection, often showing dedication by supporting their partner's dreams and aspirations. A Vulture partner offers a dynamic, intellectually stimulating, and loyal relationship that encourages mutual growth and exploration.

GAZELLE

☆ ☆ ☆

June 11–July 1

In Mesopotamian tradition, gazelles were synonymous with grace, resourcefulness, and ingenuity. Those born in this sign take risks and undertake ventures without fear, and when their gambles pay off, remarkable success is possible. Ignoring the sneers of others, Gazelles are stubborn in their convictions and determined to succeed. The Gazelle is unafraid and will tell others exactly what they think, offering a genuine and honest opinion. No malice is intended; they are just outspoken and keen to speak their minds.

Gazelles are always prepared for a new challenge; they love variety, and the unusual or unexpected is taken in their stride. This can mean that pitfalls evident to others are unforeseen by the Gazelle. People born in this sign have extreme confidence and are at their best when overcoming problems and facing difficulties. However, they struggle to pick themselves up and start over if things go wrong. Gazelles are good-natured and considerate, although of a highly charged disposition. Motivated by the urge to extract the best from life by adapting to existing conditions and creating new possibilities from very little, those born in this sign can succeed in endeavors that associates would never attempt. Nevertheless, Gazelles rarely bulldoze their way through obstacles but skillfully navigate their way around them.

Fashion sense does not come naturally for Gazelles; those born in this sign consider what they do far more important than how they look. They are prepared to dress up to suit an occasion or conform at work, but they can appear awkward doing so. Nevertheless, they are seldom unkempt and can look good in casual attire, giving them an aura of relaxed confidence. They generally have a refined taste in music and can be good dancers and graceful movers. Gazelles are accomplished socializers and are often popular. They are defensive regarding their friends and always ready to stand up to dominating, controlling, or aggressive people on their behalf.

Gazelles are imaginative, witty, and erudite. However, they can have an unusual, sometimes eccentric manner that can be annoying. Moreover, they are inclined to say exactly what they think, which may not always be what others want to hear. Luckily, most born in this sign tend to gravitate toward people with an unconventional attitude to life and can take a Gazelle's idiosyncrasies in their stride. Gazelles can be reckless, but some are unlikely to make good leaders, overlooking or unable to tell if someone is ready and prepared to follow, assuming they are just as capable as they are; the Gazelle seems unaware that others may have difficulty keeping pace. Those born in this sign do not make the best listeners; many have the annoying habit of messing with their phones or clearly having their minds on other matters when friends and colleagues need their attention.

Finances are not the Gazelle's best trait. They are often late with bills and all too willing to obtain credit they cannot afford. Those of this zodiac cycle are risk-takers, not opposed to gambling, and should think carefully before committing to schemes that offer quick ways to make money. Gazelles tend to be extravagant, and financial matters are best left to others. However, the Gazelle is inclined to be lucky, and sometimes their excesses pay off. Generous to a fault, money can burn a hole in their pockets. Individuals born under the Gazelle sign can be fearless and tenacious. They are often trailblazers with a pioneering spirit, willing to venture into uncharted seas. Their courage and boldness make them ideal candidates for taking significant risks, trying new experiences, and breaking new ground. Concerns about the past seldom bog down those born in this sign; instead, they are full of optimism and unbridled hope. They are generous and entertaining, with a good but zany sense of humor.

The Gazelle person is characterized by their dynamic energy and enthusiasm. They often take initiative and inspire others with their boldness. Their adventurous spirit drives them to seek new challenges and experiences, making them fearless. Gazelle individuals are confident and assertive, with a straightforward and honest approach to life. They are fiercely independent, valuing their freedom and autonomy. Despite occasional impatience, their determination and resilience help them overcome obstacles. They are also known for their generosity and loyalty, making them dependable friends. Their passion and zest for life make them vibrant and inspiring individuals.

Positive Characteristics

The Gazelle is forever formulating fresh ideas, is inventive and creative, and has equally artistic and technical flairs. Always looking for something new, they are prepared to take risks courageously. Those born in this sign are not easily distracted but optimistic about most endeavors. They share an emotional and romantic temperament coupled with a keen interest in the well-being of others. Most are considerate and trustworthy, with a keen sense of loyalty. Gazelles share an abundance of originality and let little stand in the way of a fruitful and exciting lifestyle. They are typically energetic and enthusiastic, with an optimistic attitude that uplifts others. Those born in the Gazelle sign have a dynamic, adventurous nature and are lively and brave. Known for their vivacious nature, they possess natural confidence and leadership ability, often taking charge. Their venturesome spirit drives them to explore new experiences. Gazelles are passionate and enthusiastic, bringing a sense of excitement to everything they do. They are highly independent, valuing their freedom and personal space. Their straightforwardness and honesty make them trustworthy companions. Gazelles are also resilient, quickly returning from setbacks with a positive attitude. Their determination and strong willpower enable them to achieve their goals and inspire those around them.

❋ Negative Characteristics

An unrealistic attitude to life can make it difficult for Gazelles to realize ambitions. Complications can arise through failure to accept problems or avoid danger. Many Gazelles have a stubborn attitude, sometimes amounting to pigheadedness. Conflict with those in authority or incompatibility in family life is often a problem. Those born in this sign tend to be extravagant with money; in business matters, mistakes are likely with investments. Most endeavors are all or nothing for the Gazelle; few born in this cycle leave anything in reserve. Being so inventive, the Gazelle can be absent-minded, forever mislaying things. There is a marked tendency for people of this zodiac sign to fail to listen, even to ignore advice by being tied up in their thoughts. Their impulsiveness often leads to rash decisions without considering the consequences. They can be impatient and easily frustrated by delays or obstacles. Gazelles may also tend toward aggression, reacting angrily when things don't go their way. Their competitive nature can make them overly combative and unwilling to compromise. Sometimes, they can be self-centered, focusing on their needs and desires above others. While appreciated in some contexts, their blunt honesty can come across as insensitive or tactless. Additionally, their independence can sometimes manifest as a reluctance to seek help or collaborate.

❋ Appearance

The Gazelle is the most expressive of signs. One of the most notable features of those born in this sign is their arms. They are long and graceful; Gazelles use them expressively in conversation, making broad and exaggerated gestures. Although they are elegant, Gazelles are not the neatest of people. Unless it is essential to dress up for an occasion, most born in this cycle are content to wear whatever is at hand. Those born in this zodiac cycle are hard to ignore; talkative and expressive, they can quickly take over an event or fill a room with their presence. When you have the Gazelle's interest, they can gaze intensely. On the contrary, if you lose their attention, they can stare into the distance, clearly thinking of something different, with no polite effort to cover it up.

Health

One problem people born in this sign share is insomnia. Few find it easy to sleep deeply or for long without waking; restless nights are typical. This is especially true if the Gazelle is engaged in a particularly absorbing enterprise. Sometimes, stress and extended periods of devoted activity can lead to headaches or migraines. Although they are quite capable and often bounce back well, the Gazelle person who has suffered a setback can sometimes fall into melancholia or even depression. Due to their adventurous nature, those born in this zodiac sign tend to suffer more than their fair share of injuries.

The Formula for Success

Gazelles have a panoramic view of the world, sharing an overall appreciation of the enterprises in which they are engaged. Few are naturally specialists, preferring to involve themselves in multiple aspects of an initiative. Although they may have various skills, Gazelles ensure that they master the most critical aspects of their work to the fullest. The typical Gazelle is always prepared to take risks to ensure success. Gazelles are the first to break new ground, and two prime traits are dedication to work and adaptability to fresh ideas. Those born in this sign are erudite and communicate well. They are imaginative and creative but work their best alone rather than as a team. The problem is they want to take the lead but do not necessarily make the best leaders. Gazelles work and live best when given the space to use their imagination. Gazelles set ambitious goals and pursue them with unwavering commitment and energy. Embracing their adventurous spirit, they are unafraid to take risks and explore new opportunities and innovative solutions. Their assertiveness ensures they take charge and make decisive actions. Gazelle's resilience generally enables them to quickly recover from setbacks, maintaining a positive attitude and relentless drive. They can build strong teams if they balance their independence with the ability to motivate and inspire others. Many born in this sign achieve remarkable success by channeling their passion and enthusiasm, which can be contagious.

Words of Advice

Exceptionally creative, the Gazelle's ideas are often unconventional and original, attracting adverse criticism from those who are less imaginative. Few Gazelles, however, will accept censure without a fight. They say what they feel and express what they believe. This may lead to conflicts that could otherwise have been avoided. Those born in this sign should learn to hold their tongues now and again and try harder to impress or flatter others, especially those from whom they may need help or assistance. For the Gazelle, what happens today is far more critical than yesterday; they desperately need change and variety. This may result in avoiding responsibility and severing ties that may later be required. Mainly, they should avoid burning the bridges they have crossed.

Suitable Occupations

Many athletes, needing to break the pain barrier repeatedly or to push themselves beyond endurance, are born in this sign. Gazelles are often groundbreakers suited for pioneering, even dangerous, fields of work. Where there is a hazard, you will find the Gazelle. Whether as firefighters, police, aid workers, or coastguards, so often, those born in this sign are prepared to put their lives on the line to help or protect others. Gazelles can make extremely successful politicians, efficiently handling the diverse skills necessary for the role. They have excellent communicative abilities and an attention-grabbing and persuasive form of expression. Few Gazelles fail to argue their point. They make successful artists and musicians, although they usually use their creative talents to disseminate a message rather than employ art for its own sake.

As managers or employers, Gazelles may not always be the best of signs; they may lead far too readily from the front and fail to offer the support and encouragement that others may need.

The Gazelle at Work

As a negotiator, the persistent Gazelle excels. Bargaining can be long and arduous, and the Gazelle is an able player in the waiting game. However, they need to control what they say. Those who believe they are getting the better of any deal with Gazelles are deluding themselves. Gazelles go through hell and high water to achieve their aims. Many Gazelles are self-made people with a highly personal style. However, headstrong emotions can send them forging ahead, and others may struggle to keep pace. Many Gazelles have eccentric personalities, which workmates will either love or hate. There is seldom room for anything in between with the Gazelle. They make great allies but formidable opponents. Successful working relations very much depend upon being on the Gazelle's good side. As a colleague, the Gazelle brings energy, enthusiasm, and a proactive attitude to the workplace. They often take initiative on projects and motivate the team with their dynamic presence. Gazelle individuals are straightforward and honest, ensuring clear communication. Their competitive nature drives them to excel, inspiring others to improve their performance. However, their impatience can sometimes lead to hasty decisions or frustration with slower processes. Despite this, their resilience and determination make them reliable in overcoming challenges. Gazelle colleagues are also supportive and willing to help, fostering a collaborative and productive work environment.

The Gazelle Parent

Gazelles are affectionate though not possessive parents. Their children are encouraged to be self-reliant and to mix freely with others. They like to be considered friends to their kids, and many children of Gazelles enjoy their parents' company throughout their lives. Gazelle parents often look forward to school vacations; they can engage themselves in organizing exciting and absorbing pastimes to enjoy with their children. Few Gazelle parents suffer from the common problem of expecting too much of their young. They may have unrealistic ambitions for themselves, but these expectations are seldom inflicted on their offspring. A Gazelle parent is energetic, enthusiastic, and deeply involved in their children's lives. They bring a sense of adventure and excitement to parenting, encouraging their kids to explore and take risks. Gazelle parents are fiercely protective and supportive, ready to stand up for their kids. They instill independence and self-confidence in their children, teaching them to be assertive and resilient. However, their impatience and occasional impulsiveness can lead to conflicts. Despite this, their passion and dedication ensure a nurturing and dynamic family environment.

The Gazelle Child

The Gazelle child is the most contrary of any sign. From an early age, they will forever disagree with teachers or parents. It is no good merely telling a Gazelle child that something simply is, because you will always be answered with questions. Many Gazelle children are hyperactive, which, coupled with their natural curiosity, can make them something of a handful. The questioning Gazelle is quick to learn, but, providing their inquisitive character is accommodated, they can be as entertaining as their adult counterparts. Many children are untidy, but Gazelles are especially so. On the positive side, they are generally concerned about the well-being of others, and few Gazelle children will be cruel or unkind. They are often sympathetic to others from infancy and are eager to help and assist. Children tend to deny responsibility and accuse a friend or sibling when in trouble. The Gazelle child, however, is usually willing to admit fault and may even take the blame on behalf of friends.

The Gazelle Friend

Gazelles are tremendously fun to be around. They share a marvelous, although unusual, sense of humor, live life to the fullest, and can be the soul of any party. They have abundant energy, love being the center of attention, and have an excellent aptitude for thinking up novel and exciting schemes. However, Gazelles can be somewhat draining—they never seem to stop. For some people, the Gazelle is best in small doses. Others who enjoy the unusual are often happiest in the company of the exciting Gazelle. The Gazelle also expects to share their problems with their friends. With most born in this sign, friendship is an all-or-nothing affair. Gazelles are quick to forgive and seldom hold a grudge—unless, that is, someone has deliberately done them harm. When Gazelles have what they believe to be a justifiable grievance, they are experts at exacting revenge. They can stir up trouble for their opponents by skillfully setting others against them while seeming to remain blameless. Gazelles might relocate frequently, often discontent with staying in one place or situation for a long time. The Gazelle may have much to say, but they hate reminiscing. They live for today and tomorrow. The past has passed, and thinking of old times has little interest for most born in this cycle. The Gazelle may not be the ideal friend for someone seeking a quiet life.

The Gazelle Partner

Gazelles find it hard to feign an interest in matters which fail to absorb them. If they are bored, they will say so. This can sometimes lead to conflicting behavior in the caring Gazelle. If compelled by circumstances to be involved in something in which they have no genuine interest, they consider it a tiresome, duty-bound responsibility. Consequently, they will carry out what is expected but ensure everyone knows exactly how they feel. It is often advisable for a partner to exclude a Gazelle from anything they have no genuine enthusiasm for. Unlike some zodiac signs who hate feeling left out, the Gazelle will happily apply themselves to something else.

The Gazelle is a complainer, especially about service at a hotel, restaurant, or store. Indeed, on occasions, especially during journeys and vacations, Gazelles can be a pain with their grouching and moaning. It is usually a good idea for a Gazelle's partner to handle reception, waiting, and serving staff—it will make things easier for everyone. A youthful and energetic spirit characterizes the Gazelle, and regarding dating and relationships, they excel in the excitement of first encounters. Enthusiastic and passionate in their relationships, those born in this sign enjoy planning dates and rendezvous, with partners finding them fun and inspiring. However, they tend to lose interest quickly and become distracted, feeling it easier to be independent rather than putting in the long-term effort relationships require. Gazelles usually need time and experience to develop better partnership skills and an understanding of when to compromise, meaning many Gazelles form stable relationships later than other signs.

SERPENT

☆☆☆

July 2–July 20

Serpents possess a strong sense of intuition, often able to accurately assess situations and people. They tend to be wise beyond their years, offering insightful advice and solutions to those around them. An air of mystery surrounds those born in this sign, making them intriguing and often enigmatic to others. Serpents tend to have a natural charm and charisma that draws people to them effortlessly. Persistence and determination are vital traits, with Serpent individuals rarely giving up on their goals. Highly independent, they prefer to carve their path and rely on themselves rather than others. Although they possess artistic flair, Serpents do not accept art for its own sake. They seek practical applications for their creations, emphasizing their preference for tangible results. Serpents may get carried away with enthusiasm but work best if they control and direct their creativity. A lack of confidence or direction may be the cause of many problems. Once they discover a balance between the down-to-earth and the imaginative, those born in this sign can accomplish outstanding achievements. Although not the epitome of patience, the Serpent has abundant creative energy.

Many Serpents have both spiritual and material aspirations. It is as though they have a foot in two worlds. Although they seek the realms of imagination, most are realists, and few are content to live in a world of make-believe. Their intuitive decisions are often implemented with firm, rational logic. Serpents are social creatures, and those born in this sign can easily handle a combination of fun and hard work. If circumstances are in their favor, Serpents can be outgoing and extroverted. Yet, if they do not have the proper support or encouragement, they are prone to withdrawal. Generally, however, they enjoy being the center of attention; even the shy Serpent wants to be noticed. Many famous artists and novelists are Serpents. Even though they may spend much time in seclusion, their work ensures their fame.

The Serpent can be a great conversationalist and an eager listener; their company is much appreciated, and they enjoy attention. Others might envy their popularity, so Serpents may have trouble making close friends. They are neat dressers, although far more concerned with personal appearance than the state of their home. It can be a complete shock for a first-time visitor to the house of someone born during this sign to find that the Serpent's living space is nowhere near as orderly as expected. Serpents are seldom fast-fire talkers, and their humor may leave something to be desired. Instead, they have a charm that usually appeals to prospective partners. Few born in this sign are boisterous or vulgar; most are refined, gracious, and sophisticated. They may play an active role in sports and leisure pursuits but perform best in a leadership or organizational capacity or as a solo competitor. They are more opposed than most signs to being ordered about. Serpents are often interested in politics, charity work, and conservation matters. They enjoy solving problems, improving what they perceive as faulty, and pushing limits. They can be activists, campaigners, and keen advocates for causes they adopt.

Serpents are known for their intellect, creativity, and independence. Their unique character marks them out; few like to be told what to do. Serpents are unpredictable, sometimes moody, and bored by small talk or vain gossip. They can come across as cold or aloof, uninterested in social interactions for their own sake. Rebels at heart, Serpents often fail to get along well with authority figures or traditional institutions. Serpents are usually generous, helpful, and not overly concerned with material success. However, they like attention and are generally happiest in the public eye. The idealistic Serpent tends to be socially and environmentally conscious. Those born in this cycle are diligent and quick learners, and their natural curiosity makes them excellent critical thinkers. However, their intense focus on a project or pastime can lead to isolation. Being unconventional in their approach to life, they can be interested in subjects like the paranormal and the unexplained, mysteries, or in spiritual pursuits. One way or the other, Serpents are always looking for new ways to approach the world. The Serpent hates monotony and the mundane, and rules and regulations can be a big hurdle for them, even if the thinking behind them is sound.

Positive Characteristics

Having natural charm, the Serpent is both expressive and theatrical. With easily stimulated emotions, they have tremendous enthusiasm for new ideas. They share an originality of thinking with a quick intellect and good memory. Serpents can learn quickly. They have a romantic temperament and a great love of travel and adventure. Those born in this sign possess several admirable traits, including ingenuity, resourcefulness, originality, imagination, and innovation. Above all, they tend to be ideas people, brimming with inspiration and capable of highly creative lateral thinking. Serpents possess good communication skills, originality, fairness, logic, and openness to new ideas. They are unafraid to speak their minds and stand up for their beliefs; they protect friends and loved ones and stand firm against injustice. Serpent-born individuals are highly resilient and can recover quickly from setbacks. They have a rich imagination and a flair for creativity, excelling in artistic and innovative endeavors. Their ability to think strategically makes them excellent planners and problem-solvers. Their strategic thinking and focus enable them to achieve their goals, often excelling in their endeavors. Despite their independence, they deeply empathize with others, understanding their emotions and perspectives. Serpents are also deeply empathetic, understanding others' emotions and offering genuine support. Flexibility and adaptability are common traits, allowing them to thrive in changing environments. Serpents are known for their passion and determination. Their loyalty is unmatched, making them dependable friends and partners. With keen intuition, they navigate complex situations with ease. Serpents possess a magnetic charisma, drawing people to them effortlessly. They are incredibly resourceful, finding innovative solutions to problems. Their resilience allows them to overcome challenges and emerge stronger. Ultimately, Serpents are powerful, dedicated, and insightful individuals.

Negative Characteristics

Impatience and intolerance often result in considerable frustration, and difficulties arise mainly through restlessness. Those born in this cycle tend to fly to extremes, and irritability can strain relationships. Serpents have strong likes and dislikes, and their emotions are easily roused. They are often impulsive by nature, and extravagance is sometimes a problem. Envy can be a Serpent trait, and jealousy needs to be controlled. When those born in this sign commit to a particular approach, it is challenging for them to consider other options. Their mysterious nature sometimes leads to excessive secrecy, making it hard for others to get close to them. Serpent individuals can sometimes be overly cautious, and their tendency to overanalyze can result in undue hesitancy. In pursuing goals, they might sometimes resort to manipulation, using their charm and intellect to influence others. People of this sign have strategic minds that can lead to overthinking, causing unnecessary stress and anxiety. Serpent independence can sometimes come off as detachment, making them seem aloof or unemotional. Their intense nature may lead to jealousy and possessiveness, causing friction with others. Serpents are known for their stubbornness, often unwilling to compromise or change their views. They can be vengeful when wronged, holding grudges for a long time. Their strong will and determination might come off as controlling or manipulative. While a strength, the Serpent's emotional intensity can sometimes lead to irritability.

Appearance

The typical Serpent has gentle features, with large, sometimes sorrowful eyes. Although alert and active, few Serpents are fidgets or rapid, erratic movers; many have a decidedly elegant bearing. The facial features of those born in this sign are particularly expressive. When annoyed, the Serpent will open their eyes wide with surprise, then frown disapprovingly. Facial features are often angular rather than rounded, with pronounced foreheads and strong jawlines. Serpents are often taller than average, some having a sinewy appearance. Whatever their physical shape, like the snake, those born in this sign tend to be graceful movers.

Health

Strangely, many Serpents have problems with their feet, and new shoes can be agonizing. They are particularly vulnerable to colds and flu, after which many suffer from lingering coughs. Bronchitis and other chest complaints are typical for Serpents. On the positive side, few suffer from digestive complaints; ulcers are rare for those born during this sign. The Serpent should be cautious of developing bad eating habits and needs to take care of their nervous system. Prone to worry, some experience disorders such as insomnia, anxiety, and depression. Those born in this cycle with a desk job or computer-based pastime, such as gaming, need constant motivation to keep fit.

The Formula for Success

The Serpent aspires to live life to the fullest. They have the enviable knack of living well, even with little money. Those born in this sign are experts at obtaining the best from most situations. Many Serpents are fortunate in monetary matters through sound intuition regarding investments. Indeed, many of the world's most successful investors are born in this sign. Serpents have a generous nature and gain much contentment by helping others. If those close to Serpents are happy, so are they. They are progressive thinkers who can often perceive opportunities others might fail to notice. Serpents achieve success through a combination of their intense focus and unwavering determination. Their keen intuition allows them to navigate challenges and seize opportunities with precision. They are strategic thinkers, meticulously planning their steps to ensure long-term success. Serpent resourcefulness enables them to find innovative solutions to problems, turning obstacles into opportunities. Their resilience helps them recover from setbacks and keep pushing forward. The Serpent's charisma and ability to build solid and loyal relationships provide a robust support network. They leverage their deep empathy to understand others, creating alliances and fostering collaboration. Their passion and drive can propel them to excellence.

Words of Advice

Serpents struggle to run their lives on simple, well-organized lines. They often find themselves in complicated predicaments due to good intentions and a tendency to expect others to act as they do. Although generous, the Serpent has a self-indulgent streak. They soon become bored if life is not filled with variety and stimulation. They may forget their obligations and migrate to new endeavors. Serpents sometimes lack willpower, needing the moral support of others to achieve success. They are susceptible to adverse opinions and may admit defeat simply because someone has told them something will fail. Although they are strongly individualistic, they are usually anything but loners. Prone to stagnation if left without support, Serpents constantly need the encouragement of friends and associates.

Suitable Occupations

Intuition, imagination, and versatility are Serpent qualities, and many born in this sign achieve the best results once they have discovered an application for these traits. Ideal occupations for Serpents are those offering scope for their artistic talents. The Serpent is one of the most imaginative signs, and many excel in all branches of the arts. Dancing, singing, acting, and drama have strong appeal. The more retiring Serpents may concentrate on painting, writing, or sculpture, which allows them to be apart from others for much of their time. Their much-needed appreciation comes via the appeal of their work. Most Serpents commit themselves to the well-being of others, so social work and health care have strong appeal. Those born in this sign can make excellent childminders or caregivers for the sick or elderly. Youth schemes and other community work appeals. Serpents make popular employers, supervisors, and managers. Few Serpents will adopt a superior attitude when dealing with subordinates. As employees, they perform best when they are allowed to get on with their work without too much interference. They can work well with others but prefer solitude, without distractions. Many Serpents seek to be self-employed.

The Serpent at Work

The Serpent can be an enigma. A shy Serpent will be strong and motivated in a crisis, whereas the tough Serpent may be a softie. Work colleagues are often surprised by the Serpent who suddenly displays abilities or talents they least expected. It is a mistake for any prospective employer to categorize the Serpent, especially during an interview. What you see is not all you get with the mysterious Serpent. Those of this cycle may not handle their affairs with the thrift of some signs, but they have a good head for profit in business matters. A wise financial instinct often makes them accurate appraisers of market trends. Whether a shop-floor worker or a business manager, the Serpent usually knows precisely how an enterprise is likely to fare. Serpents work well in teams as leaders, although they are not at their best in frontline sales. They are too easily distracted by adverse criticism of themselves or their product. Many Serpents are fascinated by information technology and are often the first to adopt new software, quickly grasping its advantages. They have excellent memories and are keen to tackle new problems head-on. Serpents make good supervisors and managers but are not good at working for others.

The Serpent Parent

Most Serpents enjoy strong family ties. In many ways, Serpent parents may be too lax with their children. They disapprove of punishment, preferring to reward their children for success rather than scold them for failure. Serpents are one of the best signs for comforting a child who has failed an examination, is having trouble at school, or is in distress. Many Serpents spoil their children rotten. They love to see them happy, sometimes ignoring the need for firmer control. Some children may take advantage of the Serpent and turn on the tears when there is something they want. They make wonderfully devoted parents but not the best of teachers. A class full of boisterous youngsters will soon learn to walk all over the accommodating Serpent. Their intuition is one of their greatest strengths, allowing them to understand and anticipate their children's needs and emotions. This intuitive ability helps them provide the proper support and guidance, often knowing what their children need even before they do. Serpent parents are also highly empathetic, offering deep understanding and compassion.

The Serpent Child

So often a gentle, loving child, the sensitive Serpent needs much encouragement to face the harsher realities of life. The romantic painting of the tearful, wide-eyed orphan, famous in Victorian times, often epitomizes the Serpent child. They are dreamers, and many have invisible childhood friends. Even those that do not will regularly talk to themselves and can spend hours playing alone. Serpent children mature later than those of other signs. Sometimes, this means that they are bullied or badgered by older children. In their teens, however, they quickly learn to stand up for themselves. Serpents are not aggressive by nature and hate physical violence. When necessary, however, they are quite prepared to meet like with like. Serpent children are incredibly creative, and many excel in the arts. The sciences, however, seldom appeal to the Serpent child. Teachers may complain about their performance in scientific subjects like math, chemistry, or physics. Few children born in this sign pay much attention to lessons they have no interest in.

The Serpent Friend

There is a mercurial quality about the Serpent that often confuses friends. Unconsciously, Serpents can adopt the attitudes, habits, and mannerisms of those with whom they are closely associated. Serpents can be popular because they can be everything to everyone. Although they enjoy flattery and attention concerning their appearance, most retain genuine modesty regarding their work. Indeed, some find it embarrassing when they are praised for their professional achievements. Again, this can confuse friends, who may wonder if they have somehow offended with a heartfelt compliment. Serpent modesty is genuine, although some of their reactions are not. They are natural actors and can feign enthusiasm for something they have no genuine interest in. The Serpent may seem riveted by your conversation despite being bored stiff. Those born in this sign are exceedingly polite and hate to offend. They have, however, no intention of going through the same experience twice. So often, casual acquaintances are bewildered when the Serpent makes an excuse not to join them for a drink. They can be passionate, open-minded, and spontaneous, occasionally willing to make great sacrifices for others. Nonetheless, it does tend to take them some time before they can fully commit to relationships. They also find it hard to apologize.

The Serpent Partner

The personal life of the Serpent would provide rich material for the romantic novelist. Falling in and out of love is a regular habit for those born to this sign. Serpents share an idealistic, sometimes unrealistic, attitude toward romance. Even if a relationship ends in disaster, they remain optimistic about future affairs. They seem to believe that love is exactly as it is in the movies. If a relationship fails to blossom, they are often profoundly hurt and usually blame themselves. Serpents, however, are not possessive lovers, and few will continue to throw unwanted attention in an ex-partner's direction. Serpents enjoy romance to the extent that marital commitments seldom come early. Though vulnerable to passing infatuation, the Serpent is capable of considerable loyalty.

Once committed, they are dedicated and steadfast, standing by their partner through thick and thin. This loyalty builds a strong foundation of trust and security within the relationship. Serpent partners are also highly intuitive, often understanding their partner's needs and emotions without them having to say a word. This intuitive nature allows for a deeper connection and understanding, fostering a supportive and empathetic relationship. Serpent partners are incredibly passionate, bringing intensity and excitement to the relationship. They are known for their determination and willpower, often pursuing their relationship goals with relentless energy. This drive and focus can inspire and motivate their partner, creating a dynamic relationship. However, Serpent partners can also be possessive and jealous, stemming from their deep emotional investment in the relationship. They may need reassurance and open communication to manage these feelings. A Serpent partner is a devoted, passionate, and intuitive companion, offering a relationship filled with depth and intensity.

CRAYFISH

☆ ☆ ☆

July 21–August 10

The crayfish, an ancient symbol of knowledge, aptly represents those born during this sign. With their logical and calculating minds, these individuals make careful plans and wait patiently for the right moment to act. Their unique blend of patience and readiness is a fascinating aspect of their character. Like the creature they are named after, they are fast movers, striking instantly when the time is right. Crayfish are dedicated and conscientious workers. They are eager to learn and quickly find practical applications for their knowledge. A Crayfish might use their knowledge of technology to streamline a work process, their understanding of human behavior to improve team dynamics, or their culinary skills to create a unique dish. Observant and with a keen eye for the minutest of details, the Crayfish seldom misses a trick. Their adaptability, a key strength, is often called upon to deal with the problems others have failed to solve, providing a sense of reassurance. They are avid readers, preferring factual rather than fictional works; the novels they do read tend to have a deep and meaningful message.

Crayfish individuals display unwavering determination and ambition. They are not easily deterred by adversity or swayed by negative opinions. Their resilience is a source of inspiration, infusing their work with enthusiasm and energy. This resilience is a key aspect of their character that often inspires those around them. They may indulge in high-spirited activities in their leisure time, but they are serious and focused during work hours. Their realism and logical thinking guide their actions rather than relying on what they perceive as lofty intuition. Whatever the Crayfish puts their mind to, they do so with an unwavering dedication. They will devote themselves exclusively to whatever they are doing, a trait that often leads to success. Those born during this zodiac sign are good at handling financial matters but may be overthrifty. Whether or not they follow fashion depends significantly on their chosen lifestyle. They dress smartly and take pride in their appearance but have no intention of laying out good money to buy trendy clothes for the sheer sake of it. However, if their work necessitates a fashionable image, they will go to considerable lengths to ensure they are second to none. Crayfish make some of the most successful people whose career is spent in the public eye or before the camera.

Although the Crayfish can be amiable, they are unlikely to involve themselves with irrelevant small talk. They can be sparing with affection, and others must appreciate their detached nature to share their time and friendship. Once they commit themselves to someone, they can be caring and loyal, seldom needy and controlling. For someone on their level, the Crayfish can make a trustworthy and entertaining friend or colleague; they are a mine of information who will most delightfully share their knowledge and experience. Crayfish are often keen on physical fitness and are usually regular visitors to the gym, leisure center, or sporting facilities, but they are much more competitors than spectators and supporters. They have little enthusiasm for events or activities in which they have no personal stake or are not directly involved. Most born in this sign are more concerned with work and practical and economic affairs than leisure activities. They tend to be good at business, perhaps even ruthless in commercial dealings. Crayfish can be a wise investor well-versed in the unwritten rules of commerce and enterprise.

Crayfish can be intense, highly observant, curious, fearless, and independent. They seldom shy away from complex tasks, questions, or situations and are often deeply interested in the existential and philosophical. For Crayfish, mysteries exist to be solved—even the mysteries of life. Perceiving subconscious connections and noticing patterns that others miss, Crayfish can excel at solving puzzles and cracking mysteries, making them great detectives. They let such intuition guide them, working with their innate logic and deductive reason and their firm appreciation of cold, hard facts. They may have an imagination and a keen interest in the mysterious or unexplained, but they are seldom given to flights of fancy, keeping their feet firmly on the ground.

One of the most defining characteristics of Crayfish is their deep connection to family and home. They value their relationships highly and often go to great lengths to nurture and protect their loved ones. Crayfish tend to be highly imaginative and creative, frequently drawn to the arts or activities that allow them to express their rich inner worlds. However, their sensitivity can sometimes lead to moodiness and an inclination to retreat into their shell when feeling overwhelmed or hurt. Despite their tough exterior, Crayfish have a soft, caring heart. They are loyal and dependable, often serving as the emotional anchors for their friends and family. Their intuition and empathy allow them to connect deeply with others, making them cherished companions who provide unwavering support and understanding.

Positive Characteristics

Crayfish have a critical outlook on life and a strong sense of responsibility. They are prepared to relax and enjoy themselves, but only at the right time and when their working day has ended. Their ambition is supported by a shrewd intellect and the ability to devote themselves exclusively to an enterprise. Observant and curious, the Crayfish is quick to learn. They are loyal to their friends and take family values seriously. Mental energy is a marked feature of those born in this sign who behave directly and decisively. Many Crayfish show considerable initiative in the handling of financial affairs. They have swift analytical minds and can solve complex problems. With strong willpower and great determination, the self-motivated Crayfish is a force to be reckoned with. Crayfish are persistent and industrious, determined to see projects through to the end, traits that are evident in both their personal and professional lives. When those born in this sign set their sights on something, they pursue it relentlessly until their objectives are achieved. Crayfish are empathetic, nurturing, and intuitive. They excel in providing emotional support and creating a loving home environment. Their loyalty and dependability make them cherished friends and family members. Creative and imaginative, the Crayfish brings a rich, compassionate perspective to their relationships and endeavors.

Negative Characteristics

A cynical temperament may restrict social activities. Often too ready to disregard the opinions of their acquaintances, arrogance is sometimes a Crayfish fault. Occasionally, Crayfish share a less than sympathetic attitude to others. They seem to think that everyone can handle adversity as easily as themselves. Crayfish also tend to take themselves too seriously, finding it hard to stand back and laugh at their mistakes. They are slow to forgive those who have offended them, and many Crayfish are inclined to hold grudges for far too long. Particularly economically minded, they are inclined to be over-thrifty and far too frugal. While loyal and accommodating to friends, the Crayfish's demeanor can abruptly change if someone should upset them. They may bear a grudge if they feel hurt or deceived, maintaining self-defeating resentment for far too long. Those born in this sign possess a stubborn streak that can harm their well-being and development. Often inflexible and set in their ways, complications due to arrogance and pigheadedness in relationships and work can impede progress.

Appearance

Crayfish are physically expressive. If they disagree, they will slice their hands through the air as if to cut the conversation dead; in anger, they will stab an accusing finger in their opponent's direction; and when they have had enough, they will thrust out their palms as if to call for silence. The crayfish is a creature that remains motionless for long periods until they speed off to avoid predators or spring into action in pursuit of prey. Similarly, those born in this zodiac sign can be calm and serene until they are ready to act—then, they are fast, efficient, and effective. At rest, Crayfish are tranquil and relaxed, but they have quick reactions and rapid movements once they are active. Many Crayfish have melodic voices possessing an almost hypnotic quality.

Health

The Crayfish is particularly prone to coughs and colds. If a flu virus is going around, the Crayfish is sure to catch it. Cold, damp weather also affects those born under this sign. They thrive in the hottest climates, but if it is chilly or wet, the Crayfish is likely to suffer. Rheumatism, arthritis, and similar complaints may be a problem for Crayfish, especially in later years. People of this zodiac cycle tend to be extremists regarding food and exercise; they might eat too much or too little, be overconcerned with health and fitness or completely neglect it. Both extremes can lead to problems, particularly gastric and dietary issues.

The Formula for Success

The Crayfish is one of the most objective signs. Those born in this cycle refuse to judge a book by its cover. They seldom, if ever, jump to conclusions. Even when dealing with someone they dislike, they will not allow prejudice to cloud their judgment. Able to ignore irrelevant faults, the Crayfish always respects and utilizes the positive traits of allies and opponents. Few Crayfish hold stern likes and dislikes. Their opinions are usually founded upon logic, not sentiment, and they exercise patience concerning most endeavors and accurately judge the right moment to act. They can also grasp the root of a problem, possessing shrewd insight into the real cause of difficulties they may face. In any enterprise, the Crayfish will weigh the odds, potential risks, and benefits long and hard before making decisions. Crayfish are forthright and astute; they have inquiring and probing minds and are remarkably self-disciplined. Crayfish succeed through their nurturing nature, emotional intelligence, and intuitive insights. By leveraging their ability to understand and empathize with others, they excel in careers that involve caregiving, counseling, and creative arts. Their dedication and loyalty foster solid and supportive relationships, personally and professionally. Crayfish benefit from creating a stable, harmonious environment where they can thrive to achieve their goals. Harnessing their imagination and creativity, they often innovate and inspire those around them. By balancing their sensitivity with resilience and setting healthy boundaries, those born in this sign can navigate challenges effectively and achieve lasting success.

Words of Advice

Crayfish can sometimes be far too cynical, refusing to believe anything that has not been proved beyond a reasonable doubt. They are unlikely to take anything at face value or on someone else's word. Crayfish should try to have a little more faith in human nature. This may not be a perfect world, but others are generally more honest than the Crayfish is prepared to give them credit. Another Crayfish trait is the need to know the detailed affairs of those around them. Sometimes, they are too inquisitive and can annoy friends, relatives, and colleagues with questioning and probing. Paradoxically, Crayfish are particularly secretive about their own lives and activities. Few will reveal their motivations, feelings, and intentions. Crayfish's patience and shrewd intuition can make them ideal for engaging in gambles and speculative ventures. However, those born in this sign generally believe anything left to chance is strictly a mug's game. The Crayfish should learn to take the occasional risk. Too much planning and not enough action can result in missed opportunities. Although their abilities to plan and formulate strategies are formidable, those of this zodiac cycle should learn to act more quickly in both practical activities and affairs of the heart. They should also let down their guard more and not be so secretive.

Suitable Occupations

Crayfish people make great entrepreneurs, managers, and supervisors. They watch and listen carefully before arriving at conclusions and only do so after considering every angle. Accordingly, they make solid judgments and usually make sound commercial decisions. Furthermore, they quickly assert authority in a firm, decisive manner. Occupations involving intricate, detailed, or complex calculations are ideal for Crayfish. They work well with figures and excel in financial careers. Architects, designers, and engineers also include many successful Crayfish. Their strong organizational skills and keen eye for detail also suits Crayfish for work involving proofreading, editing, or copywriting as well as for administration and project management roles. Many born in this sign are also found in academic and teaching occupations and anything involving investigation or research. Crayfish thrive in professions that allow them to utilize their nurturing and empathetic nature. Suitable careers include roles in health care, such as nursing, counseling, and therapy, where they can provide care and emotional support. Many Crayfish find work in the medical profession. Their creativity and intuition make them excellent artists, writers, and musicians. Careers in hospitality and culinary arts appeal to their love for creating comforting environments. Crayfish individuals also excel in education, teaching, and childcare. Their strong organizational skills and attention to detail suit them for administration and project management roles.

The Crayfish at Work

Some signs may find applying themselves to arduous tasks hard. Crayfish, however, apply themselves with remarkable dedication. They have the enviable ability to concentrate fully on whatever they are doing. Employers can always rely on the Crayfish to do their job to the best of their ability. Those born in this sign can find it difficult to socialize with people they work with. Even when they befriend them, they generally keep their working colleagues separate from their friends outside work. Crayfish approach everything with passion and determination and have a knack for understanding the underlying complexities of a situation. They thrive when working on projects in their own way and at their own pace but struggle in collective work environments. The Crayfish fosters a supportive and collaborative team environment. Highly intuitive, they excel at understanding the needs and emotions of their colleagues, making them effective leaders and team members. Their creativity and problem-solving skills enable them to find innovative solutions. However, their sensitivity can sometimes make them susceptible to stress. By setting healthy boundaries and maintaining a balanced approach, Crayfish can navigate workplace challenges effectively, contributing significantly to the success and harmony of their organizations.

The Crayfish Parent

Crayfish make responsible parents who devote much time and effort to securing their children's future. They are keen to see their children do well at school or college. The child of a Crayfish parent is often an academic achiever. They enjoy considerable parental support and encouragement from a very early age. Parents born in this sign are happy to teach their infants to read and write, while older children will benefit from Crayfish's help with homework. Although generally frugal, Crayfish parents are prepared to spend and invest in the best family computers, tablets, and phones and stock the home with books, learning aids, and educational toys. They are ready to spend their hard-earned money to ensure their children get the best start in life. Crayfish parents are compassionate and devoted to their children. They create a warm, loving home environment, ensuring their kids feel secure and cherished. They are highly protective and often go above and beyond to support their children's dreams and aspirations.

The Crayfish Child

Crayfish are studious children. They often devote more time to learning than they do to play. Indeed, they may need open encouragement to mix with other children. Many Crayfish children prefer adult company. They mature early and can stand their ground in most situations. Unlike many young people, the Crayfish child is particularly good with finances. Pocket money is unlikely to be blown at the first opportunity on trinkets and candy but saved for something more substantial. Like their adult counterparts, the Crayfish child is seldom wasteful and has a thrifty attitude toward life. Crayfish children are deeply sensitive, intuitive, and empathetic. They often form strong emotional bonds with their family and friends, seeking comfort and security in their relationships. With vivid imaginations, they enjoy creative activities like drawing, storytelling, and role-playing. Naturally nurturing, they are particularly caring for pets or younger siblings. They can be shy and reserved, needing gentle encouragement to leave their comfort zones. Their moodiness might require patience, but their affectionate and loyal nature makes them incredibly loving. A stable, supportive environment helps Crayfish children thrive, allowing their compassionate and creative qualities to blossom.

The Crayfish Friend

Although the Crayfish is a sign of confidence, many born in this cycle are wary of casual acquaintances. The Crayfish is naturally cautious, and others may need to prove themselves worthy of their trust. Furthermore, Crayfish envisage much in return for their friendship. They expect to share and share alike with their friends and hate to feel excluded from any area of their lives. Although they are dedicated workers, they also know how to have a good time. They often devote as much to entertainment as to work—an evening out is expected to be a fun-filled excursion. During social occasions, the one thing the Crayfish cannot abide by is someone talking shop. Anyone who continues an office conversation or brings up the subject of work will likely find themselves immediately cut short by an irate Crayfish. Although they will readily enjoy themselves, Crayfish do not seek to be the center of attention. The Crayfish may be self-assured, but they are also self-conscious. Few are prepared to make a fool of themselves on the dance floor or to get drunk and lose control.

The Crayfish Partner

Crayfish are seldom eager to show their feelings. They need to trust someone entirely before sharing their genuine emotions. Consequently, their partners may need to make all the first moves. Although witty and sociable, Crayfish are frequently shy regarding relationships, finding it difficult to initiate a conversation with someone they find attractive. They prefer not to make the first move, which can hinder their love life. So often, a prospective partner can be completely unaware that a Crayfish is interested in them. A Crayfish can be deeply loving, loyal, and devoted. With their intuitive nature, they often anticipate their partner's needs and feelings, offering comfort and understanding. They value stability and are committed to building a secure home environment. Crayfish partners are highly affectionate, enjoying expressions of love and creating lasting memories together. However, their sensitivity means they can be easily hurt and require reassurance. Their moodiness can be challenging, but their unwavering loyalty and caring nature make them deeply committed and attentive partners, dedicated to maintaining a strong, loving bond.

Crayfish are sensitive and committed lovers, but breakups are tough. They hate that they may have given so much of themselves only to be rejected. They seem to cope on the outside, but they may be devastated inside. A failed relationship can create an incredibly cynical Crayfish. Few continue to chase or seek the attention of an ex-partner—they have too much pride. Rejection or a breakup can negatively influence a future relationship more than it does for most signs. The Crayfish may be suspicious of a prospective partner's intentions or be restrained in the commitments they are prepared to make. It can be some time before the Crayfish has recovered sufficiently to abandon emotional inhibitions.

LION

☆ ☆ ☆

August 11–August 30

People born in this sign can be highly imaginative yet remain securely grounded and retain a firm interest in practical affairs. They may follow artistic or pragmatic pursuits, yet whichever they choose, creative and materialist attributes are both brought into play. Lions are probably the most determined of all the signs, going through hell and high water to achieve their aims. Sometimes, however, they become headstrong and forge ahead like a rampaging lion. They are graceful and self-assured in most situations, and a natural capacity to take control affords them much respect. The Lion has an air of authority but does not insist on being seen to be in command and is prepared to work behind the scenes. The task is essential to those born in this cycle, not necessarily the person who carries it out.

For the Lion, everything has its place. There is a time for work, a time for rest, and a time for play. They commit fully to each of them but dislike mixing the three. Lions will devote themselves exclusively to whatever they do, and their dedication and focus will be unwavering. They enjoy routine and keep regular habits regarding their chosen activities. Contrarily, however, they are hopelessly unpunctual regarding other people's schedules. Lions have a marvelous capacity to work hard all day, but once they have knocked off for the evening, their minds are tuned exclusively to relaxation. Without something specific to do, the Lion is content to sit for hours, watching television, messing with their phone, gaming, reading a book, or listening to music. Like a gorged lion, those of this cycle enjoy their rest and do not take kindly to being disturbed.

Lions are sophisticated dressers, although they may be given to rather unusual styles. Few born in this cycle mindlessly follow fashion; they are usually trendsetters rather than followers. Although not conservative dressers, they tend to choose quality clothing. Lions are a sign of composure, being, most of the time, assured, calm, and collected. Nevertheless, they are rarely arrogant or aloof. For the Lion, panache comes naturally. People born in this sign are seldom loners, and most enjoy being part of a group. They are happy to stand out in a crowd—not so much to stand alone. Lions cannot stand injustice and endeavor to treat everyone with respect; they are the first to offer support to those who find themselves the victims of aggression.

In Mesopotamian mythology, lions were regarded as guardians and protectors. Those born in this cycle have strong family ties; they are proud of their homes and their relative's achievements. They are the perfect providers but can be somewhat untidy in their abode. Lions prefer to keep their home and work life separate, and it is unusual to find them simultaneously socializing with friends, family, and colleagues. They may be dedicated to each of these but prefer not to mix them. The Lion is a hoarder and collector of souvenirs and memorabilia. They love to keep a record of their lives and are often keen diarists, photographers, and home video enthusiasts. They are also likely to maintain an active profile on social media. Most Lions have pet interests to fill their spare time, and gaming has a strong appeal. Those born in this sign do not like to be disturbed, growing agitated if anything disrupts their life or necessitates a change of plan.

Lions have a great sense of humor and an individual way of living. Although they have warm personalities, they can sometimes withdraw, particularly if worried or engrossed in a problem to be solved. They are happy to be the center of attention and can make great speakers, orators, and teachers, but they are also content to sit and listen. Those born in this sign excel in various academic and practical fields, but whatever Lions do, they commit to it with their hearts and souls. Creativity and passion are hallmarks of the Lion's personality. They thrive in environments where they can express themselves and showcase their talents. Lions are also generous and warmhearted, eager to support and uplift those around them. Their loyalty is unmatched, and they fiercely protect their loved ones. However, Lions can sometimes be perceived as arrogant or domineering due to their strong personalities and desire for recognition. They may struggle with criticism and tend to be stubborn, insisting on having things their way. Despite these potential pitfalls, the Lion's optimism and zest for life are infectious, making them inspiring leaders and cherished friends.

Positive Characteristics

Lions have a determined spirit and a capacity for creative thinking. They share a sympathetic and hospitable personality, their spiritual aspirations are usually well-developed, and they generally have a patient and easygoing attitude. Lions are generous, and many exhibit a romantic attitude to life. The common good is usually a high priority for Lions, who are prepared to make many sacrifices to help those around them. Lions often have a philosophical attitude to life, and most have sublime faith that good will ultimately triumph. They tend to be optimists, always seeing the positive side of a situation. Lions make good leaders and are often the best people to turn to in times of crisis. Although it may take time, those born in this sign will see things through. The Lion is an affectionate, friendly, generous sign and makes a loyal comrade and devoted partner. Those born in this zodiac cycle remain firm in their convictions and are always prepared to aid those in need. Lions have an innate ability to draw people toward them, making them the center of attention in social gatherings. This charm is complemented by their warmhearted and generous nature. Loyalty is a cornerstone of the Lion's character. They are fiercely loyal to their loved ones and stand by them through thick and thin. This loyalty makes them dependable friends and partners. Their protective nature ensures they always look out for the best interests of those they care about, often acting as a source of strength and security.

Negative Characteristics

Relationships can be made difficult by an obstinate spirit and a refusal to admit defeat when they are wrong. Lions are not so good at fitting in with the schedules of others. There is also a marked tendency to disregard their own attitudes or to offend without intent. The Lion will often consider every angle of a problem, which can lead to too much preparation and not enough action. Those born in this sign frequently fail to seize opportunities offered to them on a plate. Lions are generally good with money but can be over-thrifty, resenting the idea of splashing out on what they consider frivolous enjoyment. Although they take considerable pride in their appearance, they can be untidy, and their personal space can be a complete mess. Lions are forgetful and take too long to complete projects or even embark on them in the first place. The Lion is loyal and trustworthy; nevertheless, they are generally unreliable regarding domestic, household, and organizational matters. Lions can also be stubborn and inflexible, particularly when their ideas or plans are challenged. They have a strong sense of pride and resist accepting criticism, often seeing it as a personal attack rather than constructive feedback. This stubbornness can hinder their ability to adapt and compromise, potentially leading to conflicts in both personal and professional relationships. Another negative Lion trait is their tendency to be overly dramatic. Their natural flair for the theatrical can sometimes escalate minor issues into major dramas, causing unnecessary stress and tension. This propensity for drama can make interactions with those born in this sign emotionally exhausting for those around them. Additionally, the Lion's strong protective instincts can sometimes border on possessiveness, leading them to be overly controlling or jealous. This can strain relationships, as their loved ones may feel stifled or restricted.

Appearance

The Lion's gaze is direct and benevolent. They habitually nod knowingly when listening and adopt an understanding smile, even when disagreeing or paying no real attention. Lions move confidently; they carry their heads high and walk with their backs straight. At rest, however, Lions tend to sprawl. They seldom sit neatly in a chair, preferring to make the most of all available space and comfort. Few Lions are quick or flighty; most are slow and deliberate movers. Those born in this sign often have thick hair, and as they take great pride in their appearance, it is usually well-styled to suit their temperament. Lions are bold, graceful, and regal and move with a sense of authority. Even when they are dirty and messy following work or sport, they still have the enviable knack of making themselves look presentable.

Health

The Lion's ability to relax completely may result in weight problems. Few are worriers, and those born in this cycle are seldom concerned about their well-being. Therefore, many tend to ignore preventative medicine or tell-tale signs of illness. Repetitive strain injuries or other ailments best tackled early may be left unattended by the Lion. This can lead to complications that might easily have been avoided. Problems with the lower back and legs are more evident than other signs, but a robust immune system protects Lions from seasonal illnesses that affect others.

The Formula for Success

Lions are unafraid of failure or recrimination. They are fully prepared to be disbelieved, even ridiculed, until their point is proved. Insults or sneers have little influence on Lions, who have the confidence and self-assurance to believe they are right. Indeed, Lions seldom commit themselves to any enterprise of which they are uncertain. Those born in this cycle are prepared to persevere long and hard to achieve results. The good-natured and accommodating Lion should not be mistaken as submissive. The person who considers the Lion a pushover is in for a shock. Lions usually know precisely what they want and how to get it. They may prefer to see others happy and contented, but Lions will act forcibly and unyieldingly to prevail if another's plan conflicts with theirs. Astuteness and strength of purpose work hand in hand to make the Lion a formidable opponent.

Words of Advice

People born in this sign are protective by nature. Once something is theirs, they hate to give it up. Lions will adhere to a notion or continue with an enterprise even when outmoded or doomed to failure. They should take time to re-examine their circumstances and adjust their approach when necessary. Most endeavors will likely succeed as the Lion considers every factor before starting an enterprise. However, if the failure does result from unforeseen circumstances, the Lion can be ill-prepared. Lions should remember to keep something in reserve to avoid being left stranded. This advice is especially true in romance. Love can be an all-or-nothing affair for the Lion. If a relationship should fail, the Lion is taken entirely off guard. Although they may accept failure with dignity, it can strip them of the necessary determination to begin again. It will usually take someone or something else to spur them into action.

Suitable Occupations

Lions flourish in many trades and professions. As keen planners and organizers, they fare particularly well in commerce. An artistic Lion has tremendous insight into what is popular; advertising and the fashion world employ many born in this sign in essential positions. Lions are equally content to work behind the scenes in the entertainment world, for instance, and as many are found offstage as in the public eye. Those Lions who do perform before an audience usually do so uniquely and unusually. Lions in manual trades love seeing an enterprise develop from every stage to completion. They desire to witness the results of their contributions, so few Lions are comfortable in a closed working environment. Lions are excellent communicators and make good teachers and lecturers. They can be outstanding managers and leaders, although many born in this sign do not enjoy being hurried, preferring to take their own time making decisions. The Lion's attention to detail means that many lawyers are born in this zodiac cycle. They are natural communicators, good speakers, and excellent writers, meaning many Lions are authors, scriptwriters, and promoters. They also excel at working with computer hardware and as software designers.

The Lion at Work

Lions make considerate employers, exercising authority without becoming overbearing. They are genuinely concerned about their staff's well-being and ensure they are informed concerning all aspects of their work. Although Lions make excellent bosses, they are not the best of entrepreneurs. In management, they lack the ruthless streak sometimes necessary to make crucial judgments. Concern for their workforce is likely to preside over interests of sheer profit. They can also be slow to make decisions. Although this might be annoying, it does mean that their policies and strategies are founded on firm grounds. As employees, Lions make a positive contribution to the workforce. They are, however, inclined to side with those in difficulty, and the Lion's willingness to defend an unpopular workmate can result in friction with other staff members. Most born in this sign can be trusted. The Lion is a conscientious worker, not one to inform, tell tales, or run to the boss.

The Lion Parent

Although caring, Lion parents are inclined to treat their family almost like a business venture, sometimes acting more like fair employers than guardians. They will do much to ensure their children are well looked after but tend to concentrate more on their physical rather than emotional needs. To them, health, appearance, good manners, and practical achievements are sometimes focused on to the detriment of a child's inner needs. However, the Lion is a benevolent sign; they merely want the best for their young. Lion parents take a keen interest in their children's education and go to great lengths to ensure they have everything they need to succeed. They are always willing to spend money on extracurricular activities like music, dancing, and sports. Parents born in this sign will go the extra mile to help their kids with homework and can make learning fun and exciting.

The Lion Child

Most Lion children are relaxed in adult company, which some grown-ups may find disconcerting. They mature early, seldom act foolishly, and display a responsible and conscientious attitude toward life from a very early age. Lion children work well in class but hate doing homework. Like their adult counterparts, they feel it is time to relax once the working day ends. Although they generally excel in schoolwork, cramming is difficult, so examinations may suffer. However, their regulated lifestyle can prove extremely useful if they enter higher education. Unlike some students who may skip lectures, Lions will study long and hard from nine to five, as if they were already employed and paid to do a job. Children born in this sign tend to make excellent gamers and sportspeople. Many have superb memories and are inclined to do well in most endeavors.

The Lion Friend

Loyalty is a Lion virtue that stands undaunted in crisis. Lions will be especially staunch on a friend's behalf. They are idealists, always ready to come to the aid of others. Those born in this sign handle criticism well and seldom take offense. Accordingly, they make easygoing friends, especially for people who are outspoken or temperamental. Excitability, erratic behavior, or mood changes are taken in Lion's stride. All the Lion asks of their friends is fairness and honesty. Lions seldom hold a grudge and are quick to forgive. However, people born in this sign do not show particularly sound judgment regarding those around them. They live as if the world is ideal, believing that others will act like or be as considerate as they are. Sadly, the world is imperfect, and many Lions suffer relationship disappointments. Even though the Lion is hopeless at timekeeping and adhering to the schedules of others, if the Lion's own timetable life is disturbed, they can be left highly anxious, which can confuse friends. However, you will not always know when the Lion is upset. They may agree with your plans to disrupt their routine only to spend the rest of the day hovering near an exit or repeatedly looking at their watch.

The Lion Partner

The Lion is affectionate and protective, although not particularly romantic. They look for home comforts in a relationship rather than emotional bliss. Lions seek partners who are homely and consistent. Nevertheless, they are not the most domestic people to share a life; they can be untidy and take too long to make decisions. Conversely, they are loyal and devoted, and few cheat on lovers or have affairs. It may take some time for those born in this sign to commit to a relationship, but when they do, Lions devote themselves entirely and naturally expect their partners to do the same. Lions thrive on admiration and appreciation and seek a partner who recognizes and values their unique qualities. They are natural leaders and enjoy taking charge, which can be both a strength and a challenge in a relationship. While their confidence is inspiring, it can sometimes be domineering or inflexible. Lions have a strong sense of pride and can be sensitive to criticism, needing a partner who can navigate this with tact and understanding.

Lions can be charming and captivating, easily winning another's heart. The problem is that they often don't realize when someone is attracted to them. They can also be somewhat hard to understand as they keep their thoughts to themselves. Those born in this sign can be reserved regarding compliments. Still, they go to considerable lengths to ensure their partners have the most pleasurable dates, vacations, and weekends away. They bring warmth and excitement to a relationship, making their partner feel adored and cherished. Their natural confidence and charisma make them captivating companions who enjoy lavishing attention and affection on their partners. Lions are profoundly committed and protective, often going above and beyond to ensure their loved one's happiness and security. However, they can be stubborn and possessive, needing reassurance and admiration. A Lion partner's vibrant personality and unwavering devotion create a dynamic and fulfilling relationship filled with love and adventure.

SWAN

★ ★ ★

August 31–September 20

To the ancient Mesopotamians, swans were considered the spirit of fresh water. The celestial Swan was the guardian of springs, wells, streams, and waterfalls. Like the waterfall's misty spray, those born in this sign can be elusive. But like a well, their emotions run deep and are frequently misunderstood. They can also be likened to an active, fast-flowing stream. Energetic and individual, people born in this sign prefer to handle things their way, often mistrusting authority. Like a swan, they are both at home in the water and the air, being adaptable and natural multitaskers, efficiently handling several tasks simultaneously.

Those born under this sign are typically lively and quick-witted. They possess a strong urge to keep moving and are naturally curious, showing a keen interest in the lives of their friends, always ready to help and intervene on their behalf. Being born under one of the most curious signs, Swans dislike feeling left out. However, they are not natural followers; they have unique ways of doing things. The Swan is a mine of information. When discussing any topic, they display a remarkable ability to make it seem like they are an expert in the field. Eager to impress, some refuse to admit ignorance even when they lack knowledge. Nevertheless, the Swan is a sign of honesty, and those born in this astrological cycle tend to exaggerate rather than lie. They have a lively imagination and a remarkable talent to make life enjoyable for those around them, often entertaining others with their unique perspective on many aspects of living.

Swans are diligent workers and possess excellent organizational skills. Those born under the Swan zodiac sign are renowned for being neat and tidy. They naturally favor organization and cleanliness, often finding solace in well-ordered environments. Their living spaces are meticulously arranged, with everything in its designated place, reflecting their keen eye for detail and aesthetics. Swans take pride in maintaining a clutter-free life at home or work. Their methodical approach extends to their routines, ensuring tasks are completed efficiently and in a timely manner. This meticulous nature brings them inner peace and makes them reliable and dependable individuals in any setting.

People born in this sign are generally charming and generous with compliments, have a quick and sometimes dry sense of humor, and are always ready with a witty or relevant comment. Many Swans take a frivolous approach to life but can be sarcastic when annoyed. However, they usually prefer to avoid conflict and seldom resort to aggressive behavior. Instead, they are experts at using their words to diffuse tense situations. Swans have something of a temper but take out their frustration on inanimate objects, such as smashing a plate or snapping a pencil, finding noisy ways to express their anger and release tension.

Swans are compassionate, romantic, empathic, and sensitive. They have a natural artistic flair and use their vivid imagination to generate original and exciting ideas. They are creative and feel more centered when expressing their emotions through a preferred art form, such as music, writing, or crafts. Due to their deep feelings, Swans may also be drawn to psychology, philosophy, and spiritual pursuits. Those born in this sign are generally considerate and willing to go the extra mile to help their friends. Their imaginative and emotional nature enables them to perceive the world from a unique perspective, often making them accomplished artists and visionaries. An unconventional way of thinking and problem-solving can lead them into unusual and exciting situations. As innovators, many Swans have brought about change in the world. Those born in this cycle tend to think outside the box, leading to groundbreaking achievements, particularly in the arts and entertainment.

Individuals born under the Swan sign are known for their compassionate and loving nature. They possess a heightened emotional sensitivity, enabling them to stay attuned to people's feelings, although this also makes them susceptible to criticism. Accordingly, they often worry far too much about the opinions of others. Nonetheless, once they have made up their mind and decided to act, they put in all their effort and work tirelessly to accomplish their goals. Individuals born under this sign are generally hardworking and dedicated, seldom backing down from a challenge after committing to it. Swans possess an extraordinary ability to sense and perceive things that often go unnoticed by others. They tend to rely on their intuition rather than logic and reasoning, sometimes making impulsive decisions based on their gut instincts. Like the bird of their sign, they swim away if something feels wrong. People born under the Swan zodiac sign tend to avoid conflicts, but if pushed, they can defend themselves and their loved ones effectively.

Positive Characteristics

An active intellect and strong intuition typify individuals born in the sign of the Swan. They rely on self-determination and charm to succeed. They easily attract friends and are usually popular. A love of music and drama is evident, and their energetic personality and observant nature make them stand out. They are generally charitable and generous, although their ways can sometimes be eccentric. Swans will often lead an unconventional or even bohemian lifestyle. They are quick learners who are always eager for new experiences, making them quick to seize the initiative. The Swan typically exhibits selflessness and generosity, prioritizing the needs of others over their own. Witnessing the happiness of others brings them joy. They are compassionate and attentive to suffering, displaying care and sympathy for those in distress. They rarely harbor resentment, allowing issues to dissipate, and are readily forgiving to avoid confrontation. They have a receptive mindset and excel as attentive listeners.

Negative Characteristics

The Swan sign can be misunderstood. Some avoid commitments or responsibilities, resulting in isolation from family and friends. Due to their dislike of bureaucracy and refusal to conform to tradition, they may encounter otherwise avoidable complications. Although they often have a quick sense of humor, they tend to be cynical and lack tact when dealing with those they feel are wrong. They may come across as over-inquisitive, which can be disconcerting or annoying. Many born under this sign also tend to be too critical when it comes to the shortcomings of others and can be overly melodramatic. Swans display a vibrant imagination and inclination to be oblivious to their surroundings. Although they show empathy and support others, this can leave them open to exploitation due to their trusting nature. Their emotional depth and mood swings can be challenging to handle. Individuals born under this sign might struggle to concentrate on a single task and frequently get lost in daydreams, sometimes leading them to lose touch with reality.

Appearance

Swans are known for their fast movements; they are naturally energetic and rarely stay still. People born under this zodiac sign often make exaggerated hand gestures while speaking, even on the phone. They tend to be fidgety and restless, rarely appearing relaxed. During moments of deep thought, they may doodle with a pen or pencil or fiddle with small objects. However, they have the remarkable ability to appear graceful even when jumpy or nervous. The Swan has large eyes, and they usually have a warm, sincere, and welcoming smile. Their skin is adaptable to almost any climate and is generally in good condition. They tend to have excellent posture and rarely slouch. Even when moving quickly, they make everything appear effortless and are seldom awkward.

Health

Those born in the Swan sign can be overanxious, sometimes leading to adverse health effects; they are likely to suffer from allergies and nervous-related ailments. Swans dislike following routines and may skip meals, leading to digestive issues. On the bright side, they seldom have problems with weight. Claustrophobia is common among Swans, and they tend to avoid small and confined spaces, such as elevators or dark rooms. Swans are drawn to an extravagant way of life, often involving excessive eating, drinking, and lack of sleep. Maintaining moderate habits is the secret to their good health. Being mindful of their habits, following a well-rounded diet, engaging in moderate exercise, and getting enough rest can benefit the Swan more quickly than many signs. Many individuals born under this sign are hypochondriacs, but this means they are vigilant about potential health issues.

The Formula for Success

The love for language and communication characterizes those born in the sign of Swan. They have a natural talent for expressing themselves in a vivid and witty manner and are often avid readers. Although they have a great sense of humor, they abhor jokes at someone else's expense. As natural communicators, Swans can captivate others with their stories and anecdotes. They are also excellent speakers and entertainers who naturally encourage others. Swans love adventure and often find themselves in unusual situations where they thrive as the center of attention. Few suffer from stage fright, and Swans can make great actors and performers. People born under the sign of the Swan often have a compassionate nature, artistic talents, intuitive instincts, and creativity. They are deeply attuned to emotions and have a strong imagination, making them adept at creating and appreciating beauty in various forms. They are often romantic and devoted in relationships, placing great value on nurturing a connection that emphasizes the fantasy and magic in life. These traits frequently lead Swans to success in the creative arts, and it's no surprise that many famous actors and singers fall under this zodiac sign.

Words of Advice

The Swan is a symbol of adaptability and versatility. However, individuals born under this astrological sign tend to lack a clear sense of purpose, and concentration requires deliberate cultivation. Without proper focus, they may not maximize their talents despite possessing much creative potential. They can easily get sidetracked and fail to follow through with what they have started. Therefore, Swans should make longer-term plans and stick to them, as those born in this sign can be impulsive. They make good accountants, despite avoiding financial tasks. They also tend to be generous and charitable and may spend more than they can afford. Keeping a close watch on expenditure is advised. The Swan's natural curiosity can sometimes be taken as prying or meddlesome. Nevertheless, the Swan is curious and seldom has an ulterior motive for what may seem to some to be intrusive. Those born in this cycle are naturally empathic, but sometimes enthusiasm can overwhelm this enviable gift. At times, they need to deliberately employ it and pay more attention to the effect they are having on others.

Suitable Occupations

Those born in this sign can struggle with punctuality, finding nine-to-five jobs problematic. Conversely, they thrive when working alone, from home, or in an unstructured environment that allows them to use their imagination, vision, and creativity. Swans have keen powers of observation and are quick to learn. They are well suited for occupations that require fast reactions. However, they are not ideal candidates for work necessitating long periods of concentration. The teaching profession may appeal to people of this sign, as does anything connected with the media. They are well suited to dramatic arts; many accomplished actors and performers are born in this sign. Swans are excellent talkers and in their element as salespeople. However, they are not the best listeners and may fail to realize when falling short of persuading a potential buyer. They usually compensate by the sheer volume of work they can accomplish. Their social skills are ideal for promotion, publicity, and public relations. Swans are happier in the open or away from headquarters. As white-collar workers, they make better travelers, disliking the restrictions of the office environment. Similarly, as manual workers, they perform best on a job site. Many Swans excel in the field of hospitality and event planning.

The Swan at Work

Swans can turn their hands to most endeavors, and intricate or inventive work is appealing. Their creativity and imagination make them natural artists, musicians, and writers, while their empathy and compassion make them excellent counselors, therapists, and ideal for work in welfare. Swans are highly dynamic and can accomplish many tasks at once. In managerial roles, they take a firm stand on significant decisions. However, they are somewhat changeable on lesser issues, continually updating their strategy, which can confuse employees or fellow workers. Nonetheless, their adaptable approach usually reaps rewards. As fellow workers, Swans may not always be the most accessible people to get along with. Some may find them to be overly curious or prone to gossip. However, they can be fun and make even the most laborious tasks enjoyable.

The Swan Parent

People born under the sign of the Swan can make excellent parents, avidly participating in their children's activities. Young at heart, they love to engage in adventurous pastimes with their kids. Family vacations are always fun-filled and exciting. Swan parents often show a keen interest in their children's hobbies and pastimes, following them on social media and even learning to play the same games or sports. However, their enthusiasm can sometimes embarrass their older children, especially in front of friends. The Swan's approach to life is like that of a child in many ways. They are less restricted by the demands of adulthood than other signs and have endless imaginations. They relish spending time with their kids in play and are equally intrigued and curious about their children. Swan parents have a unique approach toward their child's upbringing. They tend to provide their offspring with everything they felt they lacked in childhood, openly encouraging them and allowing them the freedom to develop. As Swan parents often focus on the spiritual aspects of life, they may not devote enough time to their children's education, viewing it as a secondary responsibility.

The Swan Child

Children born under the sign of the Swan are quick learners. They tend to excel in school, but their restlessness can sometimes challenge teachers. While their academic abilities are usually impressive, their lack of concentration may be a recurring issue in their school reports. This is because Swans tend to understand the lesson early on, growing impatient and irritable while waiting for their classmates to catch up. Swan children are worriers, which can impact their examination results. They often overtax themselves due to their eagerness to perform well. Swans are more likely to achieve success at an early age, and many child prodigies are born during this sign. However, their success in later life depends mainly on their ability to control their tendency to switch interests frequently. Swans find it challenging to stick to anything for long, especially once it becomes routine. Children born in the sign of the Swan may have a natural inclination toward their instincts rather than logic. They may also be more interested in their dreams and fantasies than in real life. As a result, they may need help from their parents to stay grounded. They may have grandiose ideas about how life should be, but unfortunately, these ideas may not always align with reality.

The Swan Friend

Swans are known for being attracted to challenges and new opportunities, often prioritizing them over commitments. They have a peculiar habit of noticing shortcomings in others. Swans can be bogged down in small details, and arguing with them is futile as they can skillfully sidetrack and confuse the issue. Swans have many acquaintances but fewer long-term friends. Sometimes, Swans can be jealous, but it's usually short-lived as they tend to move on quickly. If someone offends a Swan, it's best to let it go, as they soon forgive and forget. Overall, the best approach with Swans is to live and let live. The Swan usually has an open mind. They take pride in their objectivity and listen to both sides of a story. This trait makes them the right people to approach for advice. They are good listeners and offer unbiased and diplomatic counsel, considering matters objectively, a talent not everyone possesses. Whether it's guidance on life, friendships, or affairs of the heart, the Swan friend usually offers sound advice to plan or make difficult decisions. Those born in this sign can remain calm and composed in stressful situations.

The Swan Partner

Swans often make better lovers than life partners, finding the daily chores of domestic life bothersome. Although they can be assertive in the workplace and when socializing, they prefer to take a back seat at home, choosing to leave running the home to their partners. Swans often seek a materialistic companion, and someone prepared to take charge and handle the household finances they prefer to avoid. Swans can move quickly from one relationship to another, although they can form a deep attachment when the right one comes along. Once they have met that person, the Swan will work hard to maintain a lasting partnership, provided their partner is willing to take on financial responsibilities and accommodate their interests. People born in this sign can take interest in fads, such as a sudden interest in a computer game or a new pastime that seems to obsess them. If a partner finds a Swan's activity annoying, it is best to give them time. They will likely lose interest soon enough and move on to something else.

People born in this sign are not easily annoyed, but when they are, they make a show of it, noisily banging furniture or slamming doors. This can be maddening for a partner who prefers a quiet life. Swans dislike being pressured, so airing objections and then dropping the subject is the best strategy their partner can adopt. They may strongly disagree at first, but later do precisely what was required of them while giving the impression that it had been their idea all along. They should be left to believe it was their idea, as Swans hate to appear influenced or to have been proved wrong. Being fun, attentive, and generous, Swans make great dates. However, they can be somewhat irritating in daily life. They take a long time to make up their minds about even the simplest things, and even when they finally decide, they may still complain about their decision.

CRANE

☆ ☆ ☆

September 21–October 11

In Mesopotamian mythology, the crane symbolized rebirth, renewal, and recovery. In ancient Babylon, it was known as the firebird, a term symbolizing its ability to rise from its ashes, much like the phoenix in later Greek and Egyptian traditions. This exotic bird is said to have made its nest of spices, and when the sun's rays set it alight, it was burned to cinders. A few days later, it was reborn, rising triumphantly from the ashes of the old. The main characteristic of those born in the sign of the Crane is the ability to create possibilities from very little. They are optimistic in the extreme, seldom accepting anything as hopeless. Usually able to find some good even in the worst situations, those born in this sign are remarkably resilient. They have a close affinity with nature and are frequently conservationists; ecology and the plight of animals are often priorities for the Crane. Possessed with a wide range of skills, those born in this zodiac cycle can enjoy success in multiple fields.

Travel holds a special allure for the Crane, who tends to prefer hot climates. They thrive in the worst heat waves, bustling about while others wilt. Hot or spicy foods are also a delight for the Crane. Conversely, they hate the cold. Cranes prefer to be active, with general television programs or casual reading not high on their list of priorities. The exceptions are sports or game shows, which the Crane may follow zealously. Those born in this sign are particularly drawn to computer games that require fast reactions, often excelling at them. Musical tastes are somewhat deep, for it is usually the meaning of a song rather than the tune that resonates with them.

The Crane thrives when their talents are not confined in one specific direction, dividing their energy between work and leisure activities. Possessing an abundance of energy, they can easily handle both. Fashion is generally unimportant to the Crane, who tends to wear the right clothes for the right occasions. The Crane is more accident-prone than many signs, usually due to haste rather than carelessness. Although they are often preoccupied with the safety of others, they tend to disregard such precautions themselves. The Crane prefers to rectify technical problems themselves before consulting an expert. Stubbornly, when the issue is beyond their ability, they refuse to quit, only to make things worse.

Wildly enthusiastic about whoever or whatever is the focus of their attention, the Crane can be oblivious to anyone or anything else. Those born in this cycle find it difficult to drag themselves away from anything they are involved in and are often late for appointments. Paradoxically, they are quick to lose patience when someone else is late. Many Cranes love sports, games, and competitions, although they are not generally attracted to team events, finding it hard to work in close harmony with others. On the other hand, they can make great team leaders. So long as teammates follow orders, the Crane is prepared to make personal sacrifices to ensure success. Cranes can naturally see multiple perspectives, making them excellent problem-solvers. They approach conflicts with a balanced viewpoint, striving to achieve equitable outcomes. However, this ability to weigh both sides of an issue can result in indecisiveness, as they may struggle to make decisions quickly, often fearing that they might upset the balance they seek to maintain. Relationships are paramount for Cranes, who prioritize companionship and connection. They are usually perceived as gracious and charming, with a knack for making others feel comfortable and valued. Their social skills are complemented by a deep appreciation for beauty and aesthetics. Cranes are often drawn to art, music, and the finer things in life, seeking to surround themselves with elegance and refinement.

Those born in the Crane sign are known for their passion, curiosity, intensity, and adaptability. They are fearless in their pursuit of knowledge and are not afraid to explore unchartered territories. They possess an insatiable thirst for knowledge and are adaptable and flexible. Cranes are natural explorers and love the freedom to wander. They can grow bored quickly and may rebel against authority, which can create conflicts in the workplace. Although they can be valuable team members, their independent streak can make them challenging to work with, as it sometimes leads to unpredictable and spontaneous behavior. They are social, charming, and value relationships, often seeking companionship and cooperation. Cranes naturally can see both sides of an issue, making them excellent mediators. However, they can sometimes struggle with indecision, as they weigh all options carefully. They appreciate beauty and aesthetics, often having a refined taste. The Crane embodies a love for peace and a quest for equilibrium.

Positive Characteristics

The Crane is resilient, optimistic, and determined and has an inventive and adaptable personality. They are dynamic and highly active, able to find new uses for the most unlikely things. Technically gifted in the crafts, this sign also shows a conscientious attitude toward work. There is a strong tendency to champion the plight of the unfortunate and an enviable power to inspire confidence and enthusiasm in others. Many born in this sign share an interest in spiritual matters, some indulging in deep philosophical thought. Others are often inspired by a Crane's ability to see the big picture and offer insightful advice to help solve their problems. Those born in this sign have the natural ability to analyze situations from all perspectives and reach practical solutions. They are highly creative and entertaining and often remarkably erudite. Cranes are known for their diplomatic and fair-minded nature. They excel in social situations, charming others with their friendly demeanor and ability to create harmony. Their strong sense of justice ensures they always strive for fairness and harmony. Cranes are great mediators, adept at seeing multiple perspectives and resolving conflicts amicably. They have a refined taste, appreciating beauty and aesthetics in all forms. Their cooperative and compassionate nature makes them wonderful friends and partners. Cranes possess a natural charm that draws people to them. Their friendly and engaging demeanor makes them popular in social settings. They are adept at making others feel comfortable and valued, often becoming the heart of social gatherings. Their conversational skills and ability to connect with various personalities contribute to their reputation as gracious hosts and delightful companions.

Negative Characteristics

The Crane has a stubborn streak. They prefer to do things their way—even when they know they are wrong. Often a dreamer, the Crane may refuse to face reality when problems occur. Too much time is spent on failed endeavors when moving on to something else may be the best course of action. The Crane is often headstrong and occasionally egotistical. They are usually straightforward and honest, but sometimes, this trait can result in misunderstandings, communication problems, and hurt feelings. However, the positive aspect is that Crane tends to have a lighthearted approach to life, which makes it difficult to stay angry with them for long. While they are usually thoughtful, they are prone to upset others unintentionally by prematurely arriving at conclusions. Cranes can struggle with indecisiveness, often weighing options excessively and delaying decisions. Their strong desire for harmony may lead them to avoid confrontations, sometimes at the expense of their own needs and opinions. This tendency to keep the peace can result in superficiality, as they may prioritize appearances over substance. Cranes might also become overly reliant on others' approval, fearing disapproval or rejection. Their quest for balance can sometimes manifest as inconsistency or lack of commitment. While they aim for fairness, this can make them appear hesitant or uncommitted in their actions and decisions.

Appearance

Those born in this sign tend to appear determined. Their penetrating, sometimes piercing gaze can be highly attractive to potential partners.

The Crane's nose is usually sharp, although the chin tends to be round. Weight is seldom a problem; abundant nervous energy generally keeps the Crane slim and agile. Many born in this sign have a cheeky demeanor and are often described as having a mischievous smile. They frequently have symmetrical facial features, soft contours, and expressive, bright eyes. Their well-shaped lips and warm, welcoming smiles add to their charm. Cranes usually have well-maintained hair, often styled elegantly, with a preference for natural shades. Their balanced physique and graceful movements reflect their inherent sense of balance. Generally, Cranes present a polished and elegant look, exuding charm and attractiveness in any setting.

Health

The Crane usually enjoys good health, although skin complaints may occur. Often, this is the result of stress. Diet is seldom a cause of concern for the Crane. They can eat almost anything without ill effects. Back problems may be in evidence due to a tendency to stoop. Cranes can be overactive and restless, so they must avoid stressful situations resulting in tension. There is a tendency to work long under extreme conditions, resulting in nervous exhaustion, skipping meals and rest, and generally poor dietary habits. Due to systematic overload, those born in this sign may feel tired and weak at times and suffer from insomnia. The Crane is generally a sign of good health; those born in this cycle are usually fit and in good shape. Because they are highly active, stress-related muscle issues, repetitive strain injury, and various trauma pains can be shared by those of this zodiac sign.

The Formula for Success

Cranes have tremendous vitality. Life is an adventure for them, although their craving for excitement may lead to tricky situations. Always eager for new experiences and ready to rise to the challenge, a Crane's life is full of surprises. So much do they endeavor to fill their lives with excitement that they sometimes forget about life's more practical matters. Others may be content to wait for opportunities, but Cranes will create their own. Indeed, they consider it their responsibility to seek new and exciting possibilities. They are never at a loss for something to do. Most born in the cycle have many talents that they can utilize simultaneously. The Crane formula for success hinges on their diplomatic skills, social charm, and a strong sense of fairness. They excel in creating harmonious environments and fostering teamwork, making them effective leaders and collaborators. Their ability to see multiple perspectives allows them to navigate complex situations and make balanced decisions. The Crane's appreciation for beauty and aesthetics helps them in creative fields, while their intellectual curiosity drives continuous learning and innovation. By leveraging their natural charm, fairness, and cooperative spirit, Cranes can build strong relationships, maintain balance, and succeed in personal and professional endeavors.

Words of Advice

Once Cranes have decided, they are firm in their convictions. The Crane, however, is a sign of action rather than words. Their ability to see all sides of an issue is a strength, but it can also lead to paralysis by analysis. They should practice making decisions confidently, trust their instincts, and remember that not every decision has to be perfect. Even if it involves some risk, action is better than remaining indecisive. The Crane's sociable and accommodating nature can sometimes lead to overcommitting. They should learn to set clear boundaries to protect their time and energy. Those born in this sign need to appreciate that it's okay to say no to requests that don't align with their priorities. Setting limits will help them maintain their equilibrium and avoid burnout. They should embrace their adventurous spirit and thirst for knowledge but remember to stay grounded and focused; additionally, they should balance their wanderlust with responsibilities to achieve their goals. While seeking freedom, it is advised they set realistic plans to turn their dreams into reality.

❋ Suitable Occupations

With an adventurous temperament, the Crane is especially suited for challenging occupations. Few Cranes work well with money, so financial matters are best left to others. Crane's enthusiasm is contagious, and a career in sales or promotion can be highly successful. Technically gifted, those born in this sign make excellent mechanics and engineers. Cranes are known for their love of movement and can quickly lose interest in work that requires them to sit at a desk for long periods. As free-spirited individuals, they are strongly inclined toward traveling and exploring new places. The best career choices for this zodiac sign involve travel, which can fulfill their wanderlust and provide them with sound financial security while allowing them the freedom to explore. Cranes thrive in occupations enabling adventure, exploration, and continuous learning. Suitable careers include travel guide, writer, journalist, photographer, and aircrew, where their love for travel and new experiences is fulfilled. They also excel as educators and researchers, given their thirst for knowledge and ability to inspire others. Sales and marketing roles, especially those involving travel, suit their outgoing and persuasive nature. Additionally, careers in philosophy, theology, or motivational speaking align with their quest for truth and meaning. The Crane thrives in dynamic environments where they can grow, explore, and share their insights with others.

❋ The Crane at Work

Happiest when working alone, the Crane is unlikely to succeed in partnership. In any working environment, colleagues should allow the Crane to do things their way. Cranes make tough but fair employers, although they may drive their employees too hard. As an employee, Crane's optimism is valuable to any workforce. However, their optimism may be frustrating if an enterprise is an apparent failure. The Crane just doesn't know when to quit. Cranes are imaginative and creative but lack foresight. Unfortunately, they can be stubborn to the extreme when they are wrong. They find it hard to change or adapt to new situations which are not of their choosing. The Crane is an active sign; few born in this cycle are naturally patient. Their answer to most difficulties is getting started and meeting problems head-on. Driving force, self-assurance, and ambition are strong Crane traits; most are usually ahead in the rat race.

The Crane Parent

Crane parents may be too ready to offer advice on teenage life but are seldom strict or overbearing. There is, though, an unrealistic expectation for those born in this sign to expect their children to be just like themselves. Cranes are usually devoted parents, ready to encourage their children and bring them up with pride. They are adventurous, open-minded, and encouraging. They inspire their children to explore the world, embrace new experiences, and seek knowledge. Their optimistic and fun-loving nature makes family life lively and engaging. They value independence and encourage their children to think freely and develop their opinions. However, their spontaneous nature may sometimes lead to inconsistency in routines and discipline. Despite this, their genuine enthusiasm and supportive attitude help foster a positive and open environment. Parents born in this sign instill a sense of curiosity and a love for learning in their children, guiding them to be openhearted and adventurous individuals.

The Crane Child

Crane children are happy to spend time in seclusion. They are not shy or reclusive but are content to play alone. The Crane child can be a handful for parents and teachers alike. From infancy, Cranes make it abundantly clear they have their own will. Boisterous in play, they may be given to tantrums if they fail to get their way. They are at their best when given the liberty to think and act for themselves. The competitive Crane spirit emerges in childhood, and most children born in this sign are keen to do well. Although many are good at sports, few succeed in team events. Individual competitions are best for the Crane child, who often excels at track and field athletics, swimming, and tennis. These children are not particularly good at caring for their possessions, and a careless streak can result in many broken toys. Crane children are unafraid to tackle a child larger or older than themselves, sometimes leading to brawls.

The Crane Friend

The Crane is one of the most robust signs, and those born in this cycle have resilient personalities. They seldom let the opinions of others deter or influence their actions, ignoring sneers or cruel remarks if something has failed. Although they see the best in most people, Cranes dislike arrogance and hate aggression. Courageously, Cranes are always ready to take risks for their friends. They are good in a crisis, usually the first to suggest a solution. Even if something seems hopeless, the Crane keeps things calm. In times of peril, those born in this sign can readily endanger their well-being for the good of others. Sympathetic to those in distress, the Crane often comes to the aid of people in trouble. Cranes make excellent companions for anyone prepared to take a back seat now and again. They are never dull, but their need for occasional solitude can be misconstrued.

The Crane Partner

Cranes speak their minds, clarifying their motives and objectives. Most people know where they stand with the Crane. Tact is not one of their attributes, however. Those of this sign tend to be forthright and outspoken. Nevertheless, they seldom lose their temper, although irritability is their usual reaction to someone who has failed to understand their motives. Cranes sometimes say more than is wise and find it challenging to apologize if they have offended without intent. Their usual form of apology is to make up for it in some way without ever explicitly saying they are sorry.

Often not as sensual in love as some signs, the Crane may appear restrained in a relationship. However, they are kind and generous. The Crane may be passionate, but romantic small talk is sometimes beyond their scope. Because of their reckless nature, Cranes can fall in love at first sight. They seldom dwell too long on any decision. Actions speak louder than words for the lover born in this sign, and many rush too readily into marriage. So long as the choice is correct, however, relationships can be long-lasting. Cranes make ideal partners as they hate domestic strife, giving way to their partner's wants rather than creating a fuss. There is usually too much else on their minds for them to become entangled in quarrels. Given their strong personalities, few people can have ambivalent feelings about a Crane. A Crane's individualism can lead to problems. However, if a partner is prepared to take the relationship on an equal footing, life can be fulfilling for both. The Crane is seldom jealous. They usually know precisely what to do if their partner appears interested in someone else. If they fail, the Crane will soon look elsewhere. After a breakup, as in most areas of their life, they prefer to take a clean break and start again.

SCORPION

★ ★ ★

October 12–November 4

In Mesopotamian tradition, the scorpion was regarded as a guardian with its sting and ambush-hunting technique. In mythology, it often appears as a treasure guardian and a shapeshifter, a metamorphic entity able to change into the form of any other creature. Similarly, those born in the cycle of the Scorpion share many characteristics with different signs. They have worldly attributes, such as a strong desire for financial security and a keen eye for investments. They also possess innovative power, often coming up with unique solutions to problems, and mental agility, allowing them to adapt to new situations quickly. This adaptability as well as their ability to modify their behavior to suit their present company and current predicament is a trait that never fails to intrigue.

In legend, the celestial Scorpion was not just a creature but a riddle to be solved. It held its secrets close within its pinchers, revealing them only to those who could decipher its puzzles. Similarly, those born during the Scorpion zodiac sign forever challenge the world around them, not antagonistically but with a sparkle in their eyes, which signifies their curiosity and thirst for knowledge. They possess a mischievous quality, often seen in their playful and witty nature, that never fails to entertain those around them. Although it sometimes bewilders others, this quality adds a unique charm to their personality.

The Scorpion was also a symbol of mystical power. Often, circumstances unfold just as the Scorpion predicted. This unusual ability is due to uncanny foresight, intuition, and an instinctive awareness that would make the Scorpion an excellent detective. Scorpions are not just great conversationalists but also eager listeners. Many people are enchanted by their eloquent manner and flamboyant personality. Their enigmatic demeanor allows them to stand out from the crowd, meaning they enjoy much attention and may be the object of jealousy. Most born in the cycle of the Scorpion are neat, with personal appearance and domestic order having high priority.

Scorpion individuals are not just enigmatic and mysterious; they also excel in social and professional settings. They take a central role in social activities and often become some of the most successful career people in business. They are always ready to give advice and comfort those in distress. It is not difficult to determine a Scorpion's mood; they seldom keep their problems to themselves and cannot keep excitement contained. There are few secrets regarding the Scorpion's state of mind.

Many born in this sign are natural performers, excellent entertainers, and at ease in company. They love to surround their lives with excitement and can adapt their character and humor to suit the occasion. The Scorpion loves to fascinate those around them and is always prepared to be the center of attention. Nevertheless, they will not let fun, entertainment, and social occasions encroach upon their professional life, dividing their time equally between business affairs and leisure activities. They can be somewhat ruthless in commercial dealings and expect competitors and rivals to be as hardened as they are. However, outside the workplace, the Scorpion is friendly, outgoing, and likes to make everything as enjoyable as possible.

Scorpions can be sparing with their heartfelt affections and expect others to share their sentiments before committing to long-lasting friendships or relationships. They can make fascinating acquaintance with those who share their lives. Scorpions are well-read and knowledgeable on many subjects and will discuss anything enlightening and entertaining. They are typically outgoing and friendly as well as the life and soul of a party. They generally have something interesting to say and are unafraid to converse deeply about life, politics, and beliefs.

Scorpions are usually curious, leading some to think they are prying. However, there will seldom be any ulterior motive for their interest; they want to get to know those around them. Scorpions are versatile and adaptable, integrating themselves into different situations and relationships. Their tendency to seek new experiences and opportunities accounts for their systematic approach to thinking and problem-solving, making them a mine of information.

Positive Characteristics

Outwardly, the Scorpion is humorous, witty, and fun-loving, but inwardly, they maintain a serious and sharp-eyed attitude to life. They are ambitious, with the capacity to exercise authority, while a strong will and conscientious attitude result in many Scorpions holding positions of responsibility. Scorpions are always optimistic concerning their chosen ventures, and a strong sense of intuition often brings them much success. Scorpions shine when engaged in conversation. With natural charm and the desirable trait of adaptability, they can get along with most people. Although they are serious, intense, and focused in their professional and working lives, they do not take themselves too seriously regarding leisure and socializing. They have considerable powers of concentration, coupled with manifold technical and artistic skills. Those born in this cycle are also highly self-disciplined, possessing the mental stamina to remain on top of most situations. Scorpions can wear many hats and put their knowledge to use in various circumstances. They have chameleon-like personalities, easily integrating themselves into different situations and relationships. They have a careful and systematic approach to problem-solving. Those born in this sign share a quick-fire wit; they are engaging and entertaining. In business, they are prepared to play the long game, waiting patiently for the right time.

Negative Characteristics

Opportunities are sometimes missed through too great an attachment to outdated ideas or methods. Scorpions tend to make errors of judgment based on firmly held opinions. Moreover, many born in this sign share unrealistic expectations, so disappointments are bound to arise. Others may consider Scorpions to be arrogant or vain at times. They may also find Scorpion intuition disturbing. Additionally, Scorpions are frequently too curious and tend to be too inquisitive concerning other people's lives, which some may find annoying, even upsetting. In times of difficulty, there is also a marked tendency for Scorpions to blame others for problems of their own making. Scorpions are known for their intelligence but can sometimes be overly analytical, leading to indecisiveness. They may struggle to make simple choices and become anxious when faced with significant decisions, such as moving or changing careers. Commitment can be challenging for those born in this sign, and their adaptability can sometimes result in impulsive behavior and difficulty sticking to their goals. They may also be inclined to cancel plans at the last minute.

Appearance

Scorpions tend to have firm features and a confident and authoritative stature. They usually have a benevolent gaze and exude an aura of self-assuredness. Those born in this zodiac cycle move with an air of certainty; they carry their heads high and walk with their backs straight. Few are quick or erratic; most are slow and deliberate movers—until they are ready to strike. Many Scorpions have a youthful and dynamic appearance that reflects their energetic and friendly nature. They have expressive and animated facial features and deep and attractive eyes. Their features are typically strong and defined, with a commanding presence that draws attention. Those of this sign usually have a composed and self-assured demeanor, often accentuated by a preference for dark or bold clothing that matches their enigmatic aura. Their physicality is frequently robust and athletic, reflecting their inner strength and determination.

Health

Scorpions are a physically active cycle, so injuries and broken limbs are more common than for some signs. They tend to ignore their well-being, so many are inclined to ignore preventative medicine or tell-tale signs of illness. Repetitive strain injuries or other ailments best tackled early may be left unattended. This can lead to complications that might easily have been avoided. Arthritis and joint problems are also common for people born during this sign. Scorpions are known for their resilience and strong constitution, often maintaining good health through sheer willpower. Scorpions should focus on activities that balance their mental and emotional well-being, such as yoga or meditation. Due to their passionate nature, they may sometimes push themselves too hard, so they need to incorporate rest and recovery into their fitness routine. A balanced diet rich in nutrients supports their overall health, helping them maintain their powerful and energetic disposition.

The Formula for Success

Scorpions are always eager for new experiences and ready to rise to any challenge. But they are careful and don't get carried away with enthusiasm, keeping a watchful eye on every detail of their ventures. They can create opportunities from very little and are one of the most enterprising signs. They are objective, refusing to judge a book by its cover, and seldom, if ever, jump to conclusions about anything before carefully examining the situation. They refuse to allow prejudice to cloud their judgment. They have patience concerning most endeavors and accurately gauge the right moment to act. Those born in this sign show an excellent capacity to grasp the root of a problem, possessing shrewd insight into the actual cause of difficulties they encounter. Scorpions are forthright and astute; they have inquiring and probing minds and are remarkably self-disciplined.

Words of Advice

Scorpions can sometimes be far too cynical, refusing to believe anything that has not been seen with their own eyes. They are unlikely to take anything at face value or on someone else's word. Those born during this sign should try to have more faith in human nature. Scorpions also feel compelled to know the detailed affairs of those around them and are sometimes far too inquisitive. They should learn to give and take more, particularly in business or professional matters. For a Scorpion, embracing balance is critical. Their intensity and passion are great strengths, but they must remember to channel them wisely. Curiosity and versatility are strengths, but the Scorpion should be mindful of scattering their energy. Communication is their forté, so they should learn to use it while practicing active listening. They need to balance their social activities with moments of solitude to recharge, but Scorpions should be careful of the tendency to overthink. They should embrace consistency and follow through on commitments to build trust and reliability in both personal and professional spheres.

Suitable Occupations

Scorpions carefully observe and listen before making decisions, considering every angle. As a result, they make well-founded judgments and sound commercial decisions. They assert authority decisively and are quick to do so. Due to their diverse attributes, Scorpions can be found in almost any occupation and quickly adapt to new roles if necessary. People born under the Scorpion sign typically pursue careers in communication, travel, and intellectual expression. These may include journalism, tourism, and the media. Scorpions are generally skillful and tactful negotiators and often excel in politics and work involving negotiations. These talents can also make them ideally suited for work in sales and marketing. Their thrifty and economically minded side means that Scorpions can make good accountants and successful business managers. Scorpions excel in careers that require intensity, focus, and a deep understanding of human nature. They thrive in investigative roles, making them excellent detectives, researchers, and psychologists. The Scorpion's passion for uncovering truths can lead to success in journalism and law. Their resilience and ability to handle pressure make them well suited for medical professions, particularly surgery.

The Scorpion at Work

Scorpions have the admirable quality of being able to fully concentrate on whatever they are doing. They can always be trusted to do any job to the best of their ability. Although they are great socializers, their propensity to keep their work and out-of-work lives separate means that many Scorpions are not natural socializers at work. Scorpions bring a unique blend of intensity, focus, and passion to the workplace. They are known for their determination and ability to see tasks through to completion, often thriving in environments that challenge them mentally and emotionally. Scorpions are highly self-motivated and possess a strong work ethic, making them reliable and dedicated employees. In leadership roles, Scorpions are strategic thinkers and natural problem-solvers. They have a keen ability to assess situations, identify underlying issues, and develop effective solutions. Their assertive and confident nature often inspires respect and loyalty among colleagues. Those born in this cycle excel in roles that require deep analysis and critical thinking, such as research, finance, and investigative positions. They are not afraid to delve into complex issues and work tirelessly until they find answers. While Scorpions can be intense and demanding, they are also intensely loyal and supportive team members. They value trust and integrity and expect the same from their colleagues. By balancing their intensity with empathy and open communication, Scorpions can foster a productive and harmonious work environment. Scorpions are diligent and determined, often becoming invaluable team members. Their resourcefulness and sharp intuition help them navigate challenges effectively. Scorpion's loyalty and focus drive them to excel in their roles, but their strong will and need for control can sometimes lead to conflicts with colleagues.

The Scorpion Parent

Scorpion parents bring fun and humor to their home. They enjoy challenging their children and are happy to participate in family games, sports, and activities. For Scorpions, conversation and debate are essential parts of family life. They enjoy reading to their children, helping them online, taking them to the park or cinema, watching television together, or playing computer games. Eager to pass on to their young ones what they know, they will endeavor to raise them to be as quick-witted, curious, innovative, and sometimes just as inquisitive as they are. Scorpion parents are deeply committed and passionate, bringing intensity to their parenting style. They fiercely protect their children, always striving to create a secure and nurturing environment. Their intuition allows them to understand their children's needs and emotions, fostering solid and empathetic connections. Scorpion parents encourage independence and resilience, often pushing their children to overcome challenges and achieve their best. However, their strong will and desire for control can sometimes lead to strictness and high expectations. Despite this, their unwavering loyalty and support make them reliable and inspiring role models, always advocating for their children's success and happiness.

The Scorpion Child

Right from infancy, Scorpion children are eager to learn. They work diligently at school and usually do well in class. Many children of this sign are born competitors. They have a constructive attitude to life, and few born in this cycle are likely to be rude, unkind, or destructive. They mix well with other children and are polite to adults, though many need constant attention and praise for their achievements. Their leadership qualities develop early; the young Scorpion often insists on leading with friends. Scorpion children are intense, curious, and perceptive. From a young age, they exhibit a strong will and determination, often surprising adults with their insight and depth of emotion. They are naturally inquisitive, seeking to understand the world around them, sometimes in ways that seem mature beyond their years. Scorpion children value honesty and are open about their feelings. They are fiercely loyal to their loved ones and form deep bonds with family and friends. Encouraging their curiosity while providing emotional support and stability helps them thrive and reach their full potential.

The Scorpion Friend

Usually, the Scorpion will read a situation perfectly. They often have tremendous insight into what is appealing and popular and can captivate their friends with original and imaginative ideas. The Scorpion is a sign of creativity and communication; many born in this cycle make the most entertaining hosts and companions. Scorpions have the versatility of character to adapt themselves to most company. Innate performing skills are a usual Scorpion trait, and many born in this sign can assume tailor-made personalities to fit readily into whatever circumstances surround them. The Scorpion has a firm sense of loyalty, and the close bond they often share with their families must be accepted by friends and lovers alike. Although Scorpions can make entertaining companions and be great people to spend time with, they can be overbearing and too curious for their own good. Nonetheless, they are loyal and devoted and always prepared to come to the aid of their friends. One negative point is that they tend to be overly thrifty and are not too keen to spend more than they must on entertainment.

The Scorpion Partner

The celestial Scorpion symbolizes insight, and most born in this cycle know precisely how to treat a prospective partner. They can readily adapt themselves to saying what others hope to hear and will act to impress. There is nothing false about this remarkable Scorpion versatility. They enjoy fitting in with others and with the spirit of an occasion. Scorpions have silver tongues, and their praise and flattery are hard to ignore. Romantics will find themselves captivated by the magnetic personality of the extroverted, self-assured Scorpion. Those born in this zodiac cycle can adapt their interests and outlooks on life to suit their lover and are often the most accommodating of partners. Scorpions hate discord in their domestic lives and will go to tremendous lengths to avoid squabbles. Unlike in work or social life, unless an argument concerns something they feel strongly about, Scorpions prefer to concede defeat for peace in a relationship.

Scorpions have a mysterious, enigmatic quality that others might love or fear. They are usually so good at whatever they turn their minds to that they can sometimes be somewhat arrogant. This is seldom hollow vanity; instead, it is an assured confidence that may be misconstrued. Like the enigmatic side of their nature, the Scorpion's assuredness is either distrusted or admired. The one thing that partners often find a problem with the Scorpion is that they want everything out in the open, don't hold back their feelings, and expect their lovers to be the same. Scorpions should realize that not everyone is as confident as they are. Scorpions also have an uncanny ability to assess a person's character quickly, even if they have just met them. They are great communicators known for their responsiveness and sensitivity as listeners. The Scorpion is versatile, can be at ease, and gets on well with most of their partner's family and circle of friends.

HORSE

★ ★ ★

November 5–November 24

In Mesopotamian tradition, the wild horse symbolized adventure. Those born in this sign are adventurous, although they retain a practical attitude to life. Their most incisive attributes arise from a remarkable aptitude to approach problems with an overall perspective. Horse sign people can often see things from everyone's point of view. They possess an alert and appealing personality. Beneath their outward calm and control, they hold a wealth of inner emotion. They have a strong sense of purpose and an innate understanding of truth and justice. Horses are fully prepared to acknowledge and rectify their mistakes, showing little reluctance in altering their ideas or tactics. They consider warranted criticism an essential part of learning and often seek the opinions of friends and colleagues.

Horses are adept at reviewing situations without personal bias and rarely take sides in conflicts. These admirable traits enable those born during this sign to devise well-balanced plans and make level-headed decisions. Horses patiently observe, listen, and learn before determining a course of action. Regardless of whether they agree with others, Horses strive to acknowledge the validity of all arguments. They are always open to being persuaded, provided the reasoning is sound. The Horse is born in the most socially versatile sign. They can converse eruditely at any level, whether in a formal setting or a local bar. They possess a firm set of ideals, no matter how unconventional they appear to others, and will defend them zealously. Horses can make devoted friends, colleagues, or partners, though they may sometimes seem distant or preoccupied. Many are changeable in temperament—one minute engrossed in conversation, the next detached in a world of thought. Acquaintances must learn to accept the Horse the way they are. Their behavior has no enmity; an idea wholly removed from the current topic may simply have occurred to them out of the blue.

Horses often adopt an unconventional style. Even those who are dedicated fashion followers or must dress formally for work will always make an individual statement in their chosen attire. Mental privacy is paramount to the Horse, who will passionately defend it. By contrast, those born in this sign are fascinated by the intentions and motivations of others. Be they friends, lovers, or mere acquaintances, Horses are determined to discover just what it is that makes people tick. They have a paradoxical, enigmatic personality that others can find enchanting.

The Horse is usually attracted to people who lead exciting or exotic lives. At the very least, people they get to know should ideally share an unusual approach to life. Horses approach everything as a task to be completed, which makes them incredibly independent and hardworking. They can achieve whatever they set their minds to, regardless of the energy required, provided they have a clear goal and a premeditated plan for getting there. Horses can hold others to high standards and are typically more conservative than some signs. They can also seem distant, emotionless, and overly analytical. They are persistent in most endeavors, such as work projects, hobbies, and domestic activities, and tend to be attentive to maintenance and repairs. In most matters, they work hard to achieve their desired results, and their determined attitude means many successful businesspeople are born in the Horse sign. Those born in this sign are always willing to learn new skills, make a concerted effort, and go the extra mile to reach their objectives.

Horses are known for their adventurous spirit and love for freedom. They possess a strong desire to explore the world, both physically and intellectually. This makes them avid travelers and perpetual learners, always seeking new experiences and knowledge. Their optimistic outlook on life often inspires those around them, bringing a sense of positivity and enthusiasm to any situation. Honesty is a hallmark of those born in this sign, though they can sometimes be blunt or tactless. They value truth and transparency and expect the same from others. Horses are also known for their philosophical nature, frequently contemplating life's more significant questions and seeking more profound understanding. In relationships, they value independence and mutual growth. They thrive with partners who share their zest for life and support their need for personal space and exploration. Overall, the Horse sign embodies a dynamic blend of curiosity, optimism, and a relentless pursuit of truth, making them one of the zodiac's most spirited and engaging signs.

Positive Characteristics

Horses share an energetic, attractive, and lively personality. A flamboyant character and a flair for the dramatic frequently assures the Horse center stage. Confident in most circumstances, the Horse has a unique talent to gain an overall perspective on any situation. A mystical inclination coupled with a highly developed sense of intuition turns many born in this sign toward philosophical or spiritual pursuits. Horses are creative thinkers who have many unique and individual ideas. They are imaginative and adaptable, and a great sense of humor affords them much social success. The Horse is highly ambitious and forever formulates admirable goals that are achieved through hard work, determination, and concerted effort. They are constantly motivated to outperform themselves and others, which drives them to continue through the necessary hardships that dedication to their pursuits may entail. Such attributes ensure that many born in this sign succeed in work and leisure activities. Many are excellent sportspeople, while others of this zodiac constellation are accomplished online gamers. Horses are natural explorers, constantly seeking new experiences and knowledge. Their optimism is infectious, bringing enthusiasm and positivity to those around them. They are honest and value truth, often speaking their mind with refreshing candor. Horses are philosophical, contemplating life's deeper meanings and inspiring others with their insights.

Their love for freedom and independence drives their pursuit of personal growth and new horizons.

Negative Characteristics

Horses have vivid imaginations; should problems become too severe, they tend to retreat into a make-believe world. Lofty ideas may reduce the chances of success in practical ventures, while unrealistic expectations are a prime source of disappointment for many Horses. Wishful thinking is also a danger in business affairs. Sometimes tactless, those born in this sign often speak their mind too readily, while their unconventional views may attract criticism. Although practical and good at maintaining their homes, a general lack of interest in laborious concerns such as financial matters can create difficulties in their domestic lives. Horses apply themselves with total commitment to most enterprises, sometimes making them obsessional and overenthusiastic, leaving friends, loved ones, and partners out of the loop. Perfectionism is a common trait for Horses, which can lead to them perceiving failure as a significant setback rather than something to overcome or move on from. Horses can remain discouraged and develop a negative outlook on their future when things don't work out for them, infecting the disposition of friends, loved ones, and work colleagues. Their honesty can sometimes be blunt, coming off as tactless or insensitive. This straightforwardness can hurt others unintentionally. The Horse's love for freedom and adventure may lead to restlessness and a fear of commitment, making them seem unreliable or inconsistent in relationships and responsibilities. While generally a strength, their optimism can sometimes result in unrealistic expectations or a tendency to overlook practical details. Additionally, their philosophical nature might make them appear detached or aloof, especially when they become absorbed in their quest for knowledge and truth.

Appearance

The Horse's eyes are wide and expressive. Many born in this sign also have high foreheads. They have quick reactions, although most move slowly or deliberately. Everything the Horse does is undertaken with an appearance of calculated accuracy. Few born in this cycle will sprawl or slouch, even when fully relaxed. Horses typically have naturally slim bodies and facial features. They have a profound and determined expression with large eyes and prominent cheek and brow bones. Horses often have a distinctive, vibrant appearance that reflects their adventurous spirit. They tend to be tall with a strong, athletic build, indicative of their love for physical activity and exploration. Their facial features are usually well-defined: a broad forehead, bright, expressive eyes, and a friendly, open smile. They often have an energetic presence and a confident, upright posture.

Health

The Horse's intense commitment to projects and endeavors may result in anxiety and other stress-related problems. However, they regulate their lives, so they are unlikely to suffer from digestive complaints or stomach trouble. Those born in this sign are often remarkably resilient. One astonishing aspect of the Horse's physiology is the capacity to heal or recover rapidly from injury. Broken bones mend quickly, and cuts and bruises disappear in no time. Those born in this sign generally possess a robust constitution and an energetic demeanor, contributing to their overall good health. Their active lifestyle and love for outdoor activities help them maintain physical fitness. However, their adventurous spirit can sometimes lead to overindulging or taking unnecessary risks, which might result in accidents or injuries.

The Formula for Success

Horses are usually honest, forthright, and idealistic. Logic and intuition direct their actions—the perfect blend for success in any undertaking. They are hardworking, blessed with a keen, intelligent mind, and have little difficulty expressing themselves clearly and eloquently. They mix well socially, are easygoing with their acquaintances, are undemanding as friends, and are helpful as colleagues. Horses display imaginative foresight and a remarkable aptitude to see things from varying perspectives. They will consider all angles of a problem before arriving at conclusions and often have inspired, fresh, and revolutionary ideas. Horses are individuals with boundless creativity and a plethora of unique ideas. Their adaptability and vivid imagination are matched only by their remarkable sense of humor, which contributes significantly to their social prowess. The Horse is marked by unwavering ambition and a propensity for setting and achieving laudable goals through steadfast determination and concerted effort.

Words of Advice

When faced with severe problems, some Horses may escape into a world of reverie or even fantasy. They may become withdrawn, secretive, and emotionally detached to avoid the harsh realities of life. Horses must confront these challenges and recognize that not everything will always turn out as hoped. Another potential challenge for individuals born under this sign is their tendency to become obsessive regarding work. When they believe in a cause, they may throw themselves into it wholeheartedly, sometimes to the detriment of their relationships, family life, and day-to-day responsibilities. The Horse must acknowledge and address this potentially disruptive aspect of their character. While their adventurous spirit and love for freedom are strengths, Horses should remember the importance of commitment and consistency. They will also benefit from cultivating tact and being more realistic when planning. Horses must maintain health by balancing physical activity with adequate rest.

Suitable Occupations

Individuals born under this sign are known for their insatiable thirst for knowledge, driving many of them to pursue academic careers where they can indulge their curiosity and passion for learning. Their inquisitive and adventurous nature also makes them well suited for roles in scientific research, where they can explore new frontiers and push the boundaries of human understanding. With a keen eye for detail and a deep appreciation for aesthetics, some individuals born under this sign find fulfillment in artistic pursuits such as photography, painting, sculpture, architecture, and commercial art. Their creative flair and attention to detail make them natural talents in these fields. Horses are often drawn to the spotlight and excel in public speaking, performance, and persuasion roles. Many successful advertising professionals and executives are born under this sign, leveraging their charisma and communication skills to thrive in their careers. In addition, their practical and mechanical inclinations make them well suited for engineering and technology-related careers, where they can apply their problem-solving abilities and innovative thinking to create and improve systems and products. Their meticulous and dedicated work ethic also translates well to computer science and information technology, where precision and accuracy are paramount.

The Horse at Work

Individuals born under the Horse sign are known for their versatile and flexible approach to work. They possess a remarkable capacity to understand and empathize with others, which makes them well suited for leadership roles. A Horse employer is characterized by their commitment to fairness, diligent work ethic, and ability to lead by example. On the other hand, a Horse employee excels in fostering positive and harmonious relationships with their coworkers. It's rare for those born under the Horse sign to get entangled in workplace conflicts, as they are adept at mediating and resolving issues fairly and justly. The ideal occupation for Horses presents them with challenges and allows them to take initiative. Horses can quickly lose interest in their work without opportunities for stimulation and creative expression. They thrive in environments that offer room for growth and personal fulfillment. It's unlikely for individuals born under the Horse sign to remain satisfied in a job that does not provide these essential elements.

The Horse Parent

Horse parents are dedicated to empowering their children to develop independent thinking skills and to be self-reliant. They have a unique ability to infuse passion and creativity into mundane school subjects, making learning an exciting experience. Unlike some parents, Horses do not impose their interests and values on their children but encourage them to explore and form their own. Additionally, Horse parents are committed to actively listening to their children, approaching their concerns open-mindedly and without prejudice before making judgments. Parents born during this astrological sign are recognized for their unwavering commitment to hard work and relentless determination to ensure a secure and comfortable life for their families. They emphasize imparting the virtues of accountability, dedication, and pragmatism to their children. These parents establish a supportive and caring atmosphere where their children can thrive, feel secure, and encounter true joy.

The Horse Child

Horse children have a remarkable sense of imagination and ambition. Their hearts are filled with high hopes, and they possess an observant intelligence and extraordinary intuition. This often leads to a strong sense of responsibility at a young age. The Horse child is constantly curious about the world around them, always seeking answers to satisfy their inquisitiveness. As a result, they may struggle with maintaining focus in a traditional classroom setting, often finding themselves lost in daydreams or gazing out the window in search of something more captivating. However, when they do apply themselves, they demonstrate immense creativity and achieve great things. While they may be able to excel in sports, physical activity is not a top priority for the Horse child. They often prefer solitary work to participating in organized group activities or team sports.

The Horse Friend

Horses steadfastly resist the pull of close-knit or exclusive communities. They dislike conformity and instead prefer maintaining a distinct yet influential presence within a crowd. While they relish social interactions and are known for their exceptional wit, humor, and love of fun, they vehemently reject the idea of adhering to a single set of standards or principles. In the Horse philosophy, everything has its place, and everyone is entitled to their opinions and lifestyle choices. While they may lean toward a somewhat conservative outlook on life, Horses are averse to dogmatic, inflexible, or stagnant individuals. They harbor a deep disdain for prejudice and any form of injustice. Those born in this zodiac sign often find it challenging to develop lasting friendships, despite their captivating and charismatic nature. Their unique perspectives and preferences make maintaining ongoing enthusiasm for typical social activities difficult. However, when they encounter someone who shares their values and beliefs, Horses can captivate and enchant their newfound companion, pulling them into a world filled with awe and adventure. Additionally, Horses are fiercely protective of their loved ones and are willing to make personal sacrifices to ensure their safety and well-being.

The Horse Partner

Horses often have high, sometimes unrealistic, expectations of their chosen partners, and as a result, they may experience disappointment. However, over time, they adapt their attitude to the realities of their relationships and find a compromise. Once committed, Horses are known to be devoted and passionate lovers, although they tend to keep public displays of affection to a minimum. Successful marriages are certainly possible for Horses if their partners respect their need for individualism and personal freedom. Horses strongly dislike interference in their affairs, regardless of the intention behind it. Occasionally, Horses may need to temporarily escape from the world and spend time alone to reflect and contemplate. During such times, they may withdraw from social interactions. Partners should understand that this is not a reflection on them, and that Horses simply need space to work through their thoughts. The Horse will soon return from their contemplative state if given the space they need.

A Horse partner is dynamic, adventurous, and full of life, bringing excitement and spontaneity to relationships. They value freedom and independence, often seeking partners who share their zest for exploration and growth. With a natural curiosity and love for learning, they enjoy engaging conversations and intellectual stimulation, making them fascinating and inspiring companions. Horses are honest and straightforward, often valuing transparency and truth above all else. While this honesty is refreshing, it can sometimes be blunt or tactless, so their partners need to appreciate and understand this trait. Their optimism and positive outlook on life are infectious, creating an uplifting atmosphere in the relationship. In love, Horses are enthusiastic and passionate, bringing a sense of adventure and excitement. They enjoy trying new things and exploring new places with their partners, making every moment together a potential adventure. However, their need for independence means they require a secure and trusting partner, giving them the space to pursue their interests and personal growth.

GOAT

☆ ☆ ☆

November 25–December 12

Those born in the Goat sign stand out for their unique blend of unwavering commitment to hard work, forward-looking perspective, and adept leadership skills. Their rare mix of self-assurance and modesty creates a comfortable environment for those around them. They are discerning in their choice of companions yet fiercely loyal and transparent. Their loyalty is a cherished trait, making those around them feel valued and appreciated. Even amid demanding schedules and high-stakes scenarios, Goats prioritize the welfare of friends. Notably, they are unafraid to provide candid feedback. When a Goat disagrees with your decisions or conduct, they won't hesitate to communicate this. What truly sets them apart is their unwavering dedication to offering pragmatic solutions and valuable guidance to help others surmount obstacles. Their proactive approach and resolute pursuit of their objectives are renowned.

The Goat personality is a complex blend of positive and negative traits. On the positive side, Goats are renowned for their exceptional work ethic, unwavering ambition, and strong sense of responsibility. They are often seen as reliable, dedicated, and determined individuals who consistently strive to succeed. However, they can sometimes be perceived as overly pessimistic, excessively focused on work, and unyieldingly stubborn. Due to their pragmatic and disciplined nature, Goats may occasionally appear distant, reserved, and overly analytical, leading others to perceive them as emotionally detached. Goats must recognize the importance of unwinding and connecting with their emotions, perhaps through meditation or introspection. Goats are inclined to hold traditional values and tend to have more conservative personalities and interests. This traditionalist approach is reflected not only in their classic sense of style but also in their character. They often prioritize stability, structure, and long-standing customs, finding comfort in the familiarity of established norms and practices.

Goats are renowned for their unyielding ambition and steadfast determination to attain their aspirations. They exhibit a remarkable work ethic and are ceaselessly driven to surpass both their expectations and those of others. This inner fortitude enables them to endure long, demanding hours dedicated to their endeavors. Goats fully anticipate and strive for rewards upon reaching the summit, whether in financial success, job security, or recognition. The Goats' work ethic and ambition make them an ideal choice when seeking a collaborative partner for a project. Their responsible and mature approach to life is palpable in their pragmatic and disciplined adherence to rules and unwavering commitment to staying organized. Goats take full accountability for their mistakes, leveraging them as opportunities for growth and ultimately transforming challenges into advantages. They exhibit exceptional proficiency in managing crucial details and are notably recognized for their discerning eye for art and design, a quality that can be genuinely appreciated.

Goats are known for their exceptional perseverance, practical approach to life, and profound sensitivity. They tackle challenges head-on and often achieve impressive success through dedication and persistence. Goats are adept at balancing their professional and personal lives, demonstrating remarkable adaptability and strong organizational skills. Their natural leadership abilities and high expectations of others are tempered by a fair and generous demeanor. In the professional sphere, Goats excel in roles such as managers and entrepreneurs due to their steadfast commitment to career advancement and results-oriented mindset. Despite their formidable exterior, Goats possess a tender and caring side, enabling them to form enduring relationships and meaningful connections with others. Individuals born under this sign are often seen as highly responsible and reliable, possessing a natural ability to lead and organize. They set long-term goals and are meticulous in their planning and execution, which often leads to significant achievements. Goats are practical thinkers who value tradition and stability, making them excellent problem-solvers in personal and professional settings.

Positive Characteristics

Goats are renowned for their unyielding resolve, perseverance, and pragmatism. They show unwavering commitment to achieving their goals and refuse to be deterred. Goats are highly motivated to demonstrate their capabilities to others and often prioritize status and symbols of success. They exemplify diligence, attaining their objectives through sheer determination and unwavering commitment. With their focused, perceptive, down-to-earth, and worldly disposition, Goats are adept at recognizing opportunities and can achieve remarkable results even when resources are limited. Many Goats are accomplished sportspeople and excel in competition. They are willing to sacrifice to achieve their goals and are reliable when completing tasks. Goats also take pride in setting high standards for themselves, allowing them to excel in leadership positions without appearing arrogant. Instead, they lead by example and maintain a humble attitude. Their practicality and resourcefulness make them excellent problem-solvers. Goats are reliable and responsible, often taking on leadership roles and ensuring tasks are completed efficiently. Their ambition drives them to achieve great success, while their patience and perseverance help them overcome obstacles. Goats are also known for their loyalty and support to friends and family. Their dry sense of humor and pragmatic outlook on life further contribute to their well-rounded and dependable nature.

Negative Characteristics

Goats are practical and down-to-earth, but this can sometimes lead them to focus on the negative in life. Their straightforward approach may cause them to miss the positive, leading to dissatisfaction and deep unhappiness. Many Goats struggle for perfection and take failure as a big disappointment. They can quickly adopt a negative attitude about their future if things are imperfect. Goats sometimes push themselves too hard. They strive to be successful and perfect, often forgetting to rest and relax. This can put a lot of stress and pressure on Goats and work against their greatest strength. Goats do well when ambitious and hardworking, but their high standards and stubbornness can be problematic, leading to unrealistic expectations. Because they stick to tradition and have a strict mindset, Goats often struggle to be open-minded and alter their perspective. Their strong drive for success sometimes leads to workaholism, causing them to neglect personal relationships. They may appear overly serious or reserved, making it difficult for others to connect with them emotionally. Due to their high standards and perfectionist tendencies, Goats can be highly critical, both of themselves and others. Their cautious nature might make them resistant to change and overly conservative. Additionally, they might struggle with pessimism, often focusing on potential problems rather than opportunities. Despite their many strengths, these traits can create challenges in their personal and professional lives.

Appearance

Goats often have a solid build and a narrow frame and adopt serious and contemplative expressions. They typically possess large, expressive eyes that convey depth and wisdom, complemented by a well-defined brow structure. Goats tend to maintain a youthful appearance as they age, often retaining their striking features well into their later years. Their smiles are known for their beauty and strength, with well-maintained teeth and a defined jawline adding to their charismatic appeal. Additionally, Goats are recognized for their prominent eyebrows and cheekbones, underlining their distinctive facial structure. Their sturdy, robust build and strong skeletal framework contribute to their enduring physical presence. Goats usually exhibit a graceful appearance and are generally short to medium height.

Health

Individuals born during the sign of the Goat are prone to experiencing knee and ligament issues. Their disciplined nature and tendency to take on too much responsibility can lead to elevated stress levels, which in turn may manifest as skin conditions, such as rashes, eczema, and hives. Their ambitious and persevering character can sometimes cause them to push their physical limits, leading to avoidable injuries. Furthermore, their independent nature may make them less likely to seek timely medical advice or recognize the importance of addressing health concerns promptly.

The Formula for Success

Goats are known for preferring traditional approaches in their professional and personal lives. They are deliberate and cautious in their decision-making, showing great patience and persistence. Goats are ambitious and set high goals, consistently striving to do better and surpass their expectations. Their responsible and mature nature and ability to stay organized enable them to overcome challenges. Goats' discipline in following the rules keeps them organized as they pursue their goals. Despite their tough exterior, Goats are also deeply sensitive but must work to be in touch with their emotions. They have a strong aversion to seeing others being put down and are quick to confront bullies and aggressors. Goats are known for their huge hearts, kindness, and loyalty. Their formula for success is rooted in their discipline, ambition, and strategic planning. They set clear, long-term goals and work diligently to achieve them, leveraging their strong work ethic and persistence. Their practicality ensures they make well-thought-out decisions, while their resourcefulness helps them overcome obstacles. Goats value structure and organization, allowing them to manage their time and resources efficiently. They are adept at learning from their experiences and continually refining their strategies. Their patience will enable them to stay focused and maintain their efforts, even in challenging times. Combined, these traits create a powerful pathway to consistent and enduring success.

Words of Advice

People born under the Goat sign must take better care of themselves and avoid overworking and overstressing. When exhausted, they must slow down and focus on their physical and emotional well-being. Goats have solid and influential personalities but must control and direct their energy to avoid getting distracted by irrelevant matters. They tend to hold grudges, which can be harmful to themselves, so learning to forgive is crucial. Goats also have quick tempers and would benefit from managing their emotions. Sometimes, they can be too outspoken and may profit from considering their opinions more carefully before expressing them. When Goats put on their blinders, it means they are overthinking something. These emotions can cause them to get stuck in a negative cycle, always assuming the worst about a situation. Goats can be overly analytical and continue to evaluate a problem for far too long. They should learn when to stop thinking and act, which can save them valuable time. Those born in this sign are particularly conservative and often hold outdated views. They should learn to take more notice of the opinions of others and be prepared to change.

Suitable Occupations

A Goat's patient and diligent nature makes them exceptionally well suited for roles in the education field, such as teaching, tutoring, and lecturing. Their innate organizational skills allow them to meticulously plan lessons, monitor and assess class progress, and manage and coordinate large groups of students with ease and efficiency. Their genuine desire to assist others in their personal and academic growth empowers them to deliver impactful and inspiring learning experiences to their students. Goats thrive in controlled environments, such as hospitals and institutions, making them ideal to work as doctors and nurses with clear patient care schedules and daily routines. Their goal-oriented nature would drive them to complete all tasks on their to-do list before taking a break or finishing their shift. Goats are known for their problem-solving abilities, organizational skills, and hardworking nature, making them well suited for jobs in the sciences. Goats excel in occupations that require discipline, organization, and strategic thinking. They are well suited for careers in finance, such as in accounting, financial analysis, or banking, where their meticulous nature and practical approach are invaluable. Due to their leadership skills and reliability, Goats thrive in management roles, including as project managers or corporate executives. Thanks to their strong sense of responsibility and ethics, they are effective in law and politics, serving as lawyers, judges, or policymakers. Additionally, engineering, architecture, and academia careers appeal to their analytical minds and methodical work styles, making them highly successful in these fields.

The Goat at Work

Goats are usually practical and disciplined. They are diligent individuals who are adept at managing finances. They enjoy optimizing and enhancing efficiency, striving to exceed expectations and achieve significant growth. Goats generally have a strong inclination toward entrepreneurship and enjoy having control over their work. They are attracted to owning and managing businesses, offering unique products and services, providing expert business consulting, giving sound financial advice, skillfully managing finances, and overseeing all aspects of operations from a leadership position. Known for their reliability and conscientiousness, Goats are eager to take on significant responsibility and are unfazed by managing substantial tasks and leading large teams of people. Goats are known for their strong desire to produce high-quality work, sometimes leading them to approach tasks slower than others. This meticulous attention to detail may cause frustration within a team, as colleagues may feel that progress is slow. This can be challenging for Goats as they often worry about how their colleagues perceive them and strive to be seen as indispensable and valuable contributors to the team.

The Goat Parent

Individuals born under this zodiac sign are deeply committed to fulfilling their parental duties. However, their strong focus on meeting their obligations may sometimes lead them to overlook the importance of spending quality time with their children and fostering a close, nurturing relationship. It's common for Goats to prioritize their career and financial responsibilities, inadvertently neglecting their children's emotional needs. As authority figures in their children's lives, they play a crucial role in imparting lessons about the value of money, the significance of being dependable, and the importance of keeping promises. However, given their high standards, they can sometimes unintentionally intimidate their children. To better balance work and play, they must infuse warmth, spontaneity, and lightheartedness into their parenting approach. By doing so, they can set a positive example for their children in demonstrating maturity, planning, and consistently working toward their goals. Additionally, they need to be mindful of being overly critical if their children's aspirations and interests differ from their own.

❋ The Goat Child

Goat children are recognized for their incredible adaptability and versatility, which empowers them to handle various situations easily. Whether navigating the demands of school, managing homework, or cultivating positive habits, children of this sign excel with minimal difficulty, owing to their natural inclination to adapt and embrace new experiences. Although they may initially exhibit some resistance, their innate flexibility enables them to acclimate to and swiftly thrive in unfamiliar environments and circumstances. Goat children demonstrate remarkable ambition, particularly in pursuing their passions and dreams. Their unwavering determination and single-minded focus make it challenging to sway their decisions, with only those closest to them privy to their innermost aspirations. Through their persistence and undivided attention, they consistently strive to surpass limitations and realize their objectives.

❋ The Goat Friend

Goats are known for their intense dedication to fostering deep, meaningful connections and treasuring their relationships with loved ones. As friends, they are incredibly supportive, offering both emotional and practical assistance while always being ready to lend a helping hand. They are great at motivating their friends to reach the highest standards and do not hesitate to provide constructive feedback when necessary. They are quick to address the shortcomings of others, which, although meant with the best intentions, can be perceived as judgmental. Goats are selective about whom they let into their inner circle, valuing honesty and loyalty in their friendships. They appreciate direct communication and aren't afraid to voice their disagreements, although they are not too good at taking criticism themselves. Nevertheless, they are quick to provide practical solutions to any problems that arise during friendships and take action to resolve any issues successfully. Goat friends are loyal, dependable, and supportive, making them invaluable companions. Known for their reliability, they are the ones you can count on in times of need, as they are always ready to lend a hand or offer practical advice. Goats are excellent listeners, providing thoughtful and honest insights without sugarcoating the truth. Their pragmatic nature ensures they approach problems with a solution-oriented mindset, helping friends navigate challenges effectively. Though they may initially appear reserved or serious, Goats possess a dry and witty sense of humor that emerges once you get to know them. They value deep, meaningful connections over superficial interactions, preferring a small circle of close friends to large social gatherings. Their high standards and discerning nature mean they choose their friends carefully, fostering relationships built on mutual respect and trust. Goats are also incredibly ambitious and goal-oriented, inspiring their friends to strive for success. However, they can sometimes be critical or appear overly cautious, but this stems from a genuine desire to see their friends succeed and avoid pitfalls. Overall, Goat friends are steadfast, trustworthy, and deeply committed to their friendships, offering a solid foundation of support and encouragement.

The Goat Partner

Individuals born under the Goat sign are known for their forward-thinking nature and a strong emphasis on creating lasting connections and forming early relationship commitments. They possess a clear life direction and are particularly attracted to individuals who share their ambitious aspirations. Goats have high standards for themselves and expect the same from their partners. While affectionate, their tendency toward perfectionism can sometimes manifest as overly critical. Goats approach dating with a serious mindset, finding it difficult to relax and savor the experience, instead focusing on evaluating the relationship's long-term potential. They often prefer to take the lead and meticulously plan dates, trips, and leisure activities, which might be perceived as overly controlling. Furthermore, Goats are creatures of habit, often establishing a regular date night and consistent routines.

Goats are known for their deep commitment to relationships, often choosing to marry or move in with their partners after dating for only a short time. Their strong intuition guides them in matters of the heart, and they demonstrate unwavering dedication to building long-term bonds with their partners. When faced with challenges at home, Goats tackle them head-on, valuing open communication and trust. However, their preference for straightforward and honest conversations may inadvertently hurt the feelings of others. Goats are highly dependable, grounded, and loyal, prioritizing the success and longevity of their relationships. Their ambitious nature and financial acumen often lead to monetary success, enabling them to be generous with gifts and to afford a lavish lifestyle. Although they can be described as straightforward, serious, and direct, Goats also possess a deeply loving and passionate side. Despite this, some friends and acquaintances may find connecting with a romantic partner born under this zodiac sign challenging.

WOLF

★ ★ ★

December 13–December 23

The Wolf has a natural talent for solving complex problems. They prefer methodical and analytical approaches, prioritizing concrete evidence over blind optimism when dealing with life's challenges. Individuals born during this sign find fulfillment in making a significant impact and consistently providing practical solutions to difficulties. If needed, their unwavering determination, a beacon of inspiration, drives them to seek a solution promptly. Wolves are recognized for their diligent and pragmatic nature, which leads them to pursue perfectionism in all aspects of their lives. This dedication to perfection is not just a trait, but a weight they carry, driving them to continuously enhance their abilities, pay attention to detail, and invest effort and time in attaining their objectives. Their meticulousness and attention to detail are distinguishing characteristics that contribute to their ability to produce high-quality results.

Wolf individuals are a study in contrasts. On the surface, they may come across as blunt, but beneath that exterior, they are inherently kind and supportive. Their conscientious nature drives them to help and support those around them, often putting the needs of others before their own. Despite their extroverted and outspoken nature, they remain modest about their achievements. They are known for their blend of practicality and imagination, approaching life with consideration and realism. They value hard work, readily dedicating themselves to projects and demonstrating unwavering commitment, even if it requires sacrifices. Their creativity manifests in various forms, such as art, dance, and writing. They exhibit a strong sense of responsibility and reliability; they are a pillar of trust in every task they take on.

Although their patience has its limits, it generally surpasses that of most individuals. They consistently seek the best in others and willingly offer their time to help. This zodiac sign is characterized by humility, love, kindness, and an eagerness to assist others. Wolves are also known for their meticulous attention to detail while maintaining the ability to see the big picture. This ability to see the big picture while not losing sight of the details is a skill and a depth of understanding. They excel at organizing and completing tasks, both for themselves and others. Their dedication to perfection can sometimes lead to dissatisfaction and fatigue, as they hold themselves to incredibly high standards and become overly self-critical and stressed when they struggle to meet them.

Favorable personality traits of the Wolf include dedication, resourcefulness, helpfulness, hard work, wit, and an endearing, often unique sense of humor. They are confident in expressing their thoughts and viewpoints. However, they can become stressed when they excessively criticize themselves and others. Challenging Wolf traits include a tendency to be self-destructive, overcritical, and self-blaming. At times, Wolves can display narcissistic tendencies, always believing they are right. However, they can also be incredibly generous, consistently offering support to their loved ones when in need. While some traits can make Wolves appear overbearing, their humor and warmth are endearing, and their charm is irresistible.

Wolves are natural mentors known for their commitment to educating and guiding others uniquely and gently. They lead by example, consistently demonstrating their high standards and attention to detail in everything they do. Wolves are celebrated for their exceptional insight and timing as well as their analytical abilities and rational approach to life. However, they often struggle with self-doubt, which sometimes holds them back from fully expressing their intuition and intellect. Despite this inner conflict, Wolves remain steadfast and deeply attuned to their senses, always considering potential risks and meticulously planning for any possible outcome in their pursuits. Creativity and imagination, linked to a grounding sense of reality, are prime traits of those born to this sign.

Positive Characteristics

Those born during the Wolf sign generally possess analytical and introspective qualities, always taking the time to carefully consider their words before speaking and thoroughly exploring any given subject before making commitments or arriving at conclusions. A greatest strength of Wolves is their ability to focus on essential details without being distracted by irrelevant information. They excel as analytical thinkers and editors, making organizing anything a natural skill. Wolves engage deeply in their creativity, utilizing forms such as art, dance, and writing as a means of expression. When entrusted with a task, they approach their responsibilities earnestly and consistently show up when needed. They tend to see the best in people and offer them the opportunity to improve their conduct when necessary. Additionally, Wolves are modest and warmhearted, consistently gentle, and always prepared to help. They have analytical minds and are highly reliable and practical, often excelling in problem-solving and organization. Their meticulous nature ensures thoroughness in everything they do. Wolves are also compassionate and supportive, always ready to help others. They have a deep sense of duty and responsibility, which makes them trustworthy and dependable friends. Their keen observational skills and intellectual curiosity constantly drive them to learn and improve. Wolves are also known for their humility and modesty, preferring to work behind the scenes without seeking the limelight.

Negative Characteristics

Individuals born under the Wolf sign are known to be extremely sensitive, and Wolves may feel offended easily, especially when they encounter setbacks in their business endeavors. When they face a setback, they tend to become pessimistic and even believe they deserve further problems. Despite being self-critical, they are not particularly fond of receiving criticism from others and are generally resistant to taking advice. Financial issues can often arise due to their tendency toward extravagance and impatience. Additionally, Wolves may be overly engrossed in their imaginative pursuits, sometimes leading to impractical outcomes. Their love for adventure can often cause them to prioritize such pursuits over more practical aspects of their lives, which may result in neglect of their responsibilities. Wolves are known to be worriers and are susceptible to experiencing anxiety when they are not actively engaged. Wolves can sometimes be overly critical of themselves and others, leading to unnecessary stress and tension. Their perfectionist tendencies may cause them to become overly meticulous, making it difficult to complete tasks efficiently. They can be excessively cautious and risk-averse, hindering spontaneity and creativity. Wolves often struggle with anxiety and worry, particularly about minor details. Their desire for control can sometimes make them appear rigid and inflexible. Additionally, they might tend to overanalyze situations, leading to indecisiveness. Their high standards can also make accepting imperfections in themselves and others challenging.

Appearance

Wolves typically have an upright posture, standing tall with confidence and assurance. They maintain direct eye contact, often accompanied by a nod of agreement and an engaging smile, even if they hold a different opinion or are momentarily distracted. Their stride—with heads held high and a robust and disciplined posture—reflects their self-assured nature. Wolves move with agility, displaying quick and decisive movements, and often exhibit fidgeting behaviors, particularly when deeply engrossed in a task. While their energy is evident in their actions, they exude a sense of grace and dignity, embodying a natural air of authority in their movements. Wolves often have a clean and polished appearance, reflecting their meticulousness and attention to detail. They tend to favor classic, understated styles, preferring quality over trendiness.

Health

The mouth and throat are the body parts most susceptible to infection; indigestion and acid reflux may also be typical. Nervous disorders can also manifest, and hypochondria is frequently observed. Nevertheless, individuals born in the Wolf sign usually enjoy good health and are generally in good shape. However, those born during this sign should be mindful of avoiding unhealthy eating habits and caring for their nervous system. Because they tend to worry, some may suffer from insomnia and anxiety. They must follow more disciplined routines, including those of a balanced diet and regular exercise, aiming for overall wellness.

The Formula for Success

Wolves are endowed with remarkable adaptability and a natural sense of humor, which allows them to thrive in various social and professional settings. Their innate acting abilities and quick wit enable them to navigate diverse situations easily. One of their exceptional qualities is their knack for inspiring others to reach their full potential. With their considerable charm and boundless creativity, individuals born during this sign often introduce innovative and unconventional ideas, although these may face pushback from those who lack vision. Nonetheless, the Wolf excels in overcoming challenges and proving their detractors wrong. They possess keen analytical skills and excel at solving complex problems. With their vivid imaginations and their ability to infuse even the most mundane tasks with excitement, they make excellent educators, entertainers, and performers, leveraging their persuasive abilities to influence and rally support for their ideas.

Words of Advice

Those born under the Wolf sign tend to thrive best when focusing on a single task at a time rather than attempting to juggle multiple issues simultaneously. This is partly due to their vast array of interests, ideas, and skills, which can sometimes make it challenging to fully commit to a single project. Wolves need to recognize and manage their tendency to be overly critical of themselves and to become less sensitive when receiving feedback. While they may be sensitive to criticism, they need to focus on their actions and be less preoccupied with the opinions of others. Additionally, Wolf individuals should control their inclination to overspend while maintaining their admirable generosity. They may benefit from being mindful of their spending habits to avoid becoming extravagant. Since managing finances might not be their forté, it could be wise for Wolves to seek assistance from a trusted individual regarding financial matters. Despite their significant talents, those born in this sign may find that business skills don't come naturally. It could benefit them to focus on developing these skills to complement their creative abilities and ensure success in their endeavors.

Suitable Occupations

Wolves are naturally inquisitive and possess strong analytical skills, making them excellent candidates for professions that require investigative and critical thinking, such as journalism. Their ability to convey information creatively and engagingly also equips them for roles in teaching. Additionally, their persuasive and imaginative nature makes sales, marketing, and advertising careers well suited for the Wolf. Their affinity for the abstract opens opportunities in various creative fields, including acting, performing arts, and music. Wolves thrive in environments that allow for short, intense bursts of work, and they dislike being constrained by strict rules and regulations. Wolves excel in occupations that require attention to detail, organization, and analytical thinking. They make exceptional researchers, scientists, and analysts due to their methodical approach and precision. As health care professionals, such as doctors, nurses, or nutritionists, their meticulous nature ensures thorough care. Wolves thrive in administrative roles, such as executive assistants or project managers, where their organizational skills shine. Their love for learning and teaching makes them excellent educators. Additionally, The Wolf's affinity for writing and communication skills suits them well for writing careers, such as jobs in editing or technical writing. Their practicality and reliability make them ideal accountants, auditors, and financial planners.

The Wolf at Work

Wolves can make excellent colleagues. They are always ready to help and offer guidance. As leaders or supervisors, they can inspire and motivate their teams with unwavering enthusiasm. Wolves are efficient, hardworking, and pay great attention to detail. They perform best when allowed to express their creativity. They have a systematic approach to their work and are knowledgeable in their fields, often pursuing hobbies related to their professions. They tend to bring work home frequently because they find it challenging to unwind and have no problem working after hours. At work, Wolves are diligent, detail-oriented, and highly organized. They excel in tasks requiring precision and analytical thinking. Their reliability and strong work ethic make them valuable team members. Wolves often take on leadership roles, ensuring projects are completed efficiently and to high standards while maintaining a supportive attitude.

The Wolf Parent

People born under the Wolf sign are known for their exceptional parenting skills. They are dedicated to their children's learning and development, prioritizing kindness and empathy over strict discipline. They believe in fostering mutual respect and take the time to explain their decisions to their children. Leading by example, these parents consistently model courteous and thoughtful behavior for their children to emulate. Wolf parents are attentive and supportive, understanding their children's needs and striving to raise well-adjusted individuals. They provide a nurturing environment and encourage a well-rounded lifestyle that includes sports, arts, and academic pursuits. They aim to make these experiences enjoyable and enriching for their children. Wolves are loving yet not possessive parents who promote independence and social interaction in their children. They prefer to be seen as friends by their kids, and many children of Wolves maintain a close bond with their parents throughout their lives. Wolf parents eagerly anticipate school breaks, using the time to plan enjoyable and engaging activities to share with their children. Few parents born in this sign exhibit the common tendency to place unrealistic expectations on their children, as they tend to reserve such high standards for themselves.

The Wolf Child

A Wolf child is often characterized by innate curiosity, intelligence, and keen attention to detail. They strongly desire to learn and understand the world around them from a young age. This natural inquisitiveness makes them excellent students who enjoy academic challenges and thrive in structured learning environments. They are likely to excel in subjects that require precision and analytical thinking, such as math and science. Wolf children are typically organized and responsible, often displaying these traits early on. They enjoy creating order in their surroundings, whether tidying up their room or arranging their toys in a specific way. This need for structure and routine helps them feel secure and in control, reducing anxiety from uncertainty. Despite their practical nature, Wolf children have a sensitive side. They are empathetic and caring, often showing concern for the well-being of others. This can make them excellent friends who are always ready to offer help and support. However, their sensitivity also means they can be easily hurt by criticism or perceived failures. Parents and caregivers need to provide constructive feedback gently and encouragingly, helping them build resilience without undermining their self-esteem. Wolf children may sometimes struggle with perfectionism. Their high standards can lead to frustration when things don't go as planned or when they make mistakes. Encouraging them to see errors as learning opportunities rather than failures can help mitigate this tendency. Teaching them the value of flexibility and adaptability is crucial for their personal growth.

❋ The Wolf Friend

Wolf individuals make fantastic companions due to their constant flow of fresh ideas and enjoyable company. With their offbeat sense of humor, they can live life to the fullest and always enliven any social gathering. Their broad range of interests and experiences equips them with a treasure trove of knowledge, making them excellent conversationalists. Nevertheless, Wolves can sometimes be challenging, as they speak without thinking. Those born under this sign relish being the center of attention and thrive by devising innovative and thrilling plans. Many people appreciate their nonconformist nature and find their company delightful, while others may find Wolves overwhelming. The Wolf is known for their mysterious and ethereal nature, which makes them stand out. They have a remarkable ability to tune into the thoughts of others with astonishing accuracy and respond appropriately. Their insights are often deeply rooted, and their instincts are reliable. However, it's important to note that they tend to change their plans at the last minute. Despite being romantic, they may struggle to remember essential dates such as birthdays and anniversaries. If they overlook a significant commitment, it's crucial not to perceive it as a personal affront or a deliberate omission. People born during this sign possess a romantic and idealistic view of relationships, often holding high expectations of their friends.

❋ The Wolf Partner

Individuals born under the sign of Wolf are often characterized by a unique trait of being unaware of their attractiveness to potential partners. This often results in them being surprised when someone expresses interest in them. Unfortunately, this natural attribute is occasionally misconstrued as disinterest on the part of the Wolf. However, their reluctance to initiate a romantic relationship usually stems from their tendency to be self-critical rather than a lack of confidence. Despite their propensity to worry excessively and, at times, hesitate to act, Wolves are generally warm and emotionally expressive once they find the right partner. Those born under this sign are renowned for their captivating personalities but are typically focused on their careers and not in a hurry to marry or settle down. Additionally, they take great care to truly understand someone before fully committing to them. Loyalty is a hallmark of the Wolf in a relationship, ensuring that one relationship has concluded before considering another. They do not shirk responsibilities to a previous partner or knowingly engage in a relationship with someone already committed.

Wolves are known for their romantic idealism, often painting a picture of love reminiscent of what is seen in movies. They tend to maintain a positive outlook on future romantic endeavors, even after experiencing a difficult breakup. However, when relationships don't unfold as they hope, they can feel deeply wounded and tend to blame themselves. Despite this, Wolves are not possessive partners and usually do not pursue their ex-partners once a relationship has ended. They have a strong appreciation for romance, which may lead them to postpone making serious commitments. While they are susceptible to temporary infatuation, Wolves can demonstrate significant loyalty. Wolves try hard to avoid causing emotional pain to others and may find it challenging to end relationships.

FISH

☆ ☆ ☆

December 24–January 14

One of the most defining traits of the Fish is their profound empathy. They have an innate ability to sense and understand the emotions of those around them, often absorbing and reflecting these feelings as if they were their own. This deep emotional sensitivity makes them exceptionally compassionate and kindhearted. They are naturally drawn to helping others, often finding themselves in roles that require caregiving or emotional support. Their friends and loved ones frequently turn to them for comfort and understanding, knowing that the Fish's empathy is genuine and boundless.

The Fish's intuition is another significant aspect of their character. Those born in this sign are perhaps the most intuitive of the zodiac, possessing a psychic-like ability to perceive underlying truths and emotions. Fish rely on their gut feelings and instincts, which are usually remarkably accurate. This intuitive prowess allows them to navigate complex social dynamics and understand people profoundly, often sensing what others need before they realize it themselves.

Creativity and imagination are hallmarks of the Fish personality. Many Fish find expression through artistic endeavors such as writing, painting, music, and dance. Their art often reflects their emotional depth and unique perspective on life, captivating audiences with its sensitivity and beauty. This creative energy is not limited to the arts but extends to problem-solving and innovation. Fish can think outside the box, coming up with imaginative solutions to challenges in all areas of life.

Despite these strengths, the Fish's heightened sensitivity can also be a source of vulnerability. They are prone to becoming overwhelmed by the emotions and energies they absorb from others, leading to feelings of melancholy or anxiety. This susceptibility can make it difficult for them to maintain emotional boundaries, sometimes resulting in a sense of being lost or confused about their identity. Fish might retreat into their dream worlds or cope with escapist behaviors. Those born in this zodiac cycle can be torn between reality and fantasy, logic and emotion, selflessness and self-preservation. This duality can sometimes make them seem contradictory or indecisive as they struggle to balance their complex inner lives with the demands of the external world. However, this duality also endows them with a remarkable capacity for adaptability and resilience, allowing them to navigate life's ups and downs with grace and flexibility.

Fish are known for their loyalty, devotion, and romanticism in relationships. They seek deep, soulful connections and are often idealistic in their views of love. This idealism can sometimes lead to unrealistic expectations, causing disappointment when reality falls short of their dreams. Nevertheless, their unwavering commitment and genuine affection make them loving and supportive partners. They willingly go to great lengths to make their loved ones happy, often prioritizing their partner's needs over their own. This selflessness, while admirable, can sometimes lead to an imbalance in relationships, as Fish may struggle to assert their own needs and desires.

The Fish's altruistic nature extends beyond their personal relationships. They have a strong sense of social justice and are often moved by the suffering and injustices they see in the world. This compassionate concern can drive them to engage in humanitarian efforts, whether through direct action, advocacy, or creative expression. Many Fish are drawn to careers that allow them to make a positive impact, such as health care, counseling, social work, or the arts.

Spirituality is another key component of the Fish's character. They are often drawn to spiritual or mystical pursuits, seeking to understand the deeper meaning of life and their place within the universe. This spiritual inclination can manifest in various ways, from traditional religious practices to more eclectic or New Age beliefs. For many Fish, their spirituality is a source of strength and comfort, providing a sense of connection to something greater than themselves. Despite their many positive traits, they can sometimes struggle with practical matters. Their dreamy nature and preference for intuition over logic can make dealing with mundane tasks and responsibilities challenging. They may struggle to stay organized, manage their time effectively, or make concrete plans. This can lead to procrastination or reliance on others to handle practical details. Developing strategies to ground themselves and enhance their practical skills can help Fish better balance their dreams and reality.

The duality of Fish also plays out in their approach to conflict. On the one hand, their empathetic and nonconfrontational nature makes them excellent peacemakers who seek harmony and avoid disputes whenever possible. On the other hand, their sensitivity means they can be deeply hurt by criticism or conflict, leading them to withdraw or become passive-aggressive. Learning to assert themselves and communicate openly about their feelings can help Fish navigate disputes more effectively and maintain healthier relationships.

Fish individuals are also known for their adaptability. Like water, they can flow and adjust to various situations and environments. This flexibility allows them to thrive in diverse circumstances and to connect with a wide range of people. However, it can also make them susceptible to being influenced or manipulated by stronger personalities. Establishing clear boundaries and developing a strong sense of self can help Fish maintain their integrity while still remaining open and adaptable.

The Fish character is a fascinating blend of empathy, intuition, creativity, and spirituality. Their deep emotional sensitivity and compassionate nature make them invaluable friends and partners, capable of providing profound support and understanding. However, their dreamy and idealistic tendencies can sometimes lead to challenges in navigating the practical aspects of life and maintaining emotional boundaries. By embracing their strengths and addressing their vulnerabilities, those born during this sign can harness their unique qualities to create meaningful and fulfilling lives.

Positive Characteristics

Fish are known for their profound empathy, allowing them to understand and connect with others' emotions. This makes them compassionate, always ready to lend a listening ear and offer genuine support. Intuition is another hallmark of Fish. They possess an almost psychic ability to sense underlying truths and easily navigate complex social situations. This intuitive nature often guides them in making wise decisions and understanding people on a deeper level. Creativity also flows naturally in Fish. They are dreamers with vivid imaginations. Their artistic talents often manifest in music, writing, painting, or other creative pursuits, captivating audiences with their expressive and emotive work. Fish are also known for their adaptability. Like water, they can seamlessly adjust to different environments and situations, displaying remarkable resilience. This flexibility allows them to thrive in diverse circumstances and connect with a wide range of people. The altruism and selflessness of Fish are commendable. They are often driven by a desire to help others, making significant contributions through acts of kindness and humanitarian efforts. These positive traits make Fish a cherished and inspiring presence in any setting.

Negative Characteristics

Fish empathy can sometimes turn into emotional overwhelm. By absorbing others' emotions too deeply, Fish may struggle to distinguish their own feelings from those around them, leading to confusion and stress. Another notable issue is their tendency toward escapism. Faced with harsh realities, Fish might retreat into their own world, rather than addressing issues head-on, leading to prolonged difficulties. Fish idealism, particularly in relationships, can result in unrealistic expectations.

They often envision perfect scenarios and may become disillusioned when reality falls short. This can lead to disappointment and a sense of betrayal, impacting their emotional well-being and relationships. Indecisiveness can arise from a reticence to make different choices and struggle to commit to a single path. This indecision can hinder their progress and create frustration for themselves and others. The Fish's selflessness, while generally positive, can lead to self-neglect. They may prioritize others' needs over their own, potentially causing burnout and resentment. Balancing their compassionate nature with self-care is crucial for their overall well-being.

Appearance

More than other signs, those born in the sign of the Fish convey emotions through physical gestures. During times of disagreement, they make sharp movements, seemingly trying to end the conversation abruptly. When angry, they exhibit a pointing gesture as if to accuse; when they've reached their limit, they extend their palms outward as if to signal for silence. This intriguing behavior sets these individuals apart. They are also known to remain perfectly still for extended periods, only to dart off swiftly—as if to evade predators or pursue their prey. Similarly, those born under the Fish zodiac sign may possess a tranquil and composed nature, often staying calm until they decide to act. They become remarkably swift, efficient, and highly productive at that point. When at rest, the Fish exhibits a quiet and relaxed demeanor, yet it can demonstrate rapid, agile movements once it becomes active.

Health

The Fish is highly susceptible to respiratory issues, including coughs and colds. They are particularly vulnerable to flu viruses and prone to infection when they are widespread. Their well-being is greatly affected by heat. While they thrive in cool, even cold climates, they risk suffering in hot or humid environments. As they age, Fish are more likely to develop conditions such as rheumatism and arthritis. Allergies, including hay fever and asthma, are common for those born during this sign due to their highly active immune system. Many Fish also experience skin rashes caused by reactions to dust, fur, and certain foods, while issues with the knees and lower back are frequently reported.

The Formula for Success

The Fish represents objectivity in the original zodiac. Individuals born under this sign are reluctant to judge a situation based solely on appearances. They rarely draw hasty conclusions and strive to maintain impartiality even when dealing with people they don't like. Rather than focusing on flaws, the Fish recognizes and utilizes the positive qualities of both allies and adversaries. They tend not to have strong preferences; their viewpoints are typically based on logic rather than emotion. Additionally, they demonstrate patience in most situations and can discern the underlying causes of challenges. Fish carefully evaluate the risks, benefits, and probabilities of any undertaking when making decisions. They are direct, perceptive, and possess a disciplined and inquisitive mindset. The Fish formula for success lies in harnessing their intuitive, compassionate, and creative nature. They should: Embrace their deep empathy to connect meaningfully with others, fostering strong relationships and collaborations. Utilize their vivid imagination and artistic talents to innovate and solve problems creatively. Trust their intuition in decision-making, as it often guides them toward the right path. Balance their emotional sensitivity with resilience, learning to navigate challenges without becoming overwhelmed. Stay adaptable, allowing their flexible nature to thrive in changing environments. Prioritize self-care to maintain their emotional well-being, ensuring they remain energized and focused on their goals.

Words of Advice

Fish, known for their empathetic nature, are often the pillars of strength for their friends and confidants. However, it's important for them to recognize their strength and set boundaries to protect their emotional well-being. Learning to say no when needed and prioritizing their own needs are not signs of weakness but of self-awareness and self-care. Grounding techniques can help them stay connected to reality, while their artistic talents can be a powerful source of inspiration and motivation. Creative activities, whether painting, writing, music, or any other art form, can be deeply therapeutic and fulfilling. While escapism may be tempting, Fish should try to face challenges directly by breaking them down into smaller, manageable steps and dealing with them one at a time. Seeking support from trusted friends or a therapist can also provide them with the strength to handle difficult situations. The Fish's selflessness is admirable, but they must remember that caring for themselves is equally important as helping others. Engaging in activities that bring joy and relaxation and practicing self-compassion is essential. Those born under this sign should trust their gut feelings and balance them with rational thought when making decisions.

Suitable Occupations

People born during the sign of the Fish are well suited for roles that involve caregiving and creativity. They excel in nursing, counseling, therapy, writing, music, painting, and acting due to their compassionate nature, understanding of others' emotions, vivid imagination, and emotional depth. Fish individuals are drawn to helping others and making a positive impact, making careers in social work, charity organizations, and humanitarian efforts highly fulfilling. In addition, roles such as yoga instructors, spiritual advisors, or holistic healers align well with the Fish's intuitive and empathetic nature. Teaching and mentoring also allow them to share their knowledge and compassion, fostering growth and inspiration in others. Individuals born in the Fish zodiac sign are often well suited for careers in finance and investment due to their uncanny intuition. They also make good publicists and commonly hold positions in public relations. Academic and teaching occupations, as well as roles involving investigation or research, are also common.

❋ The Fish at Work

In professional settings, Fish are highly valued for their unique blend of empathy, creativity, and intuitive insights. Their innate ability to deeply understand and connect with others often positions them as the emotional linchpin within team interactions. This enables them to foster a sense of camaraderie and empathy that contributes to a harmonious and supportive work environment. The Fish's creative talents set them apart, particularly in roles that demand innovative thinking and artistic expression. They shine in brainstorming sessions, consistently offering fresh and original perspectives on various projects. Additionally, their intuitive nature allows them to anticipate potential obstacles and opportunities, thereby enhancing strategic planning and problem-solving initiatives. It is worth noting, however, that individuals with the Fish personality may encounter challenges when faced with practical tasks and deadlines, as their inclination toward dreaminess can impact their focus. As such, they are at their best in flexible, collaborative work environments that allow them to leverage their strengths rather than in rigid, high-pressure settings.

❋ The Fish Parent

Fish parents are known for their unwavering dedication and responsible approach to nurturing their children. They invest significant time and effort into ensuring their children have a successful future. Their enthusiasm for their children's academic achievements is evident in how they actively support and encourage their children's educational pursuits, whether in school or college. Children of Fish parents often excel academically, benefiting from the abundant support and encouragement they receive from a young age. Those born under the sign of Fish take pleasure in initiating their young into the world of literacy and numeracy, and they continue to provide guidance and assistance with homework as their children grow older. Despite being generally prudent with their finances, Fish parents are willing to invest in high-quality family computers and stock their homes with many books, educational toys, and learning materials. Their willingness to allocate resources demonstrates their commitment to providing their children with the best possible foundation for success in life. A Fish parent's intuition is one of their greatest strengths, guiding them in making wise and empathetic decisions. They create a harmonious home life, valuing open communication and emotional support. Their nurturing and loving approach helps their children grow into compassionate, creative, and emotionally intelligent individuals.

The Fish Child

The Fish child is often a dreamer with a vivid imagination. They are gentle, compassionate, and highly intuitive, picking up on the emotions of those around them with remarkable sensitivity. Fish children are naturally creative and tend to excel in artistic pursuits, such as drawing, music, or storytelling. Their creativity knows no bounds. They are also known for their deep sense of empathy and kindness. A Fish child will often go out of their way to help others, showing a level of compassion that is mature beyond their years. Fish children can be prone to daydreaming and might struggle with more rigid, structured environments that stifle their creativity. They thrive in nurturing and flexible settings where their imaginative minds can flourish. A Fish child is a dreamer, full of imagination and creativity. They often lose themselves in their own world, filled with fantasy and wonder. They are gentle and affectionate, forming deep bonds with family and friends. Encouraging their artistic talents, whether in music, art, or storytelling, helps them thrive. Due to their sensitivity, they may need extra support to navigate challenges and build resilience. Nurturing their dreams and providing a loving, stable environment allows a Fish child to flourish.

The Fish Friend

The Fish's natural empathy makes them excellent listeners and confidants, always ready to offer a supportive word when needed. Fish friends are known for their creativity and imagination. They bring a unique perspective to any conversation, often infusing it with their artistic flair. Whether it's suggesting a new movie, recommending a book, or planning a creative outing, their ideas are always inspiring and engaging. This creativity extends to their problem-solving skills, making them valuable allies when facing challenges. Loyalty is a hallmark of a Fish friend. Once they form a bond, they are incredibly devoted and will stand by their friends through thick and thin. They are nonjudgmental and accepting, creating a safe space where their friends feel valued and understood. However, their deep emotional nature means they can be easily hurt, so they appreciate friends who are considerate and gentle with their feelings. Fish friends are often seen as the peacemakers in their social circles. They have a natural aversion to conflict and strive to maintain harmony. Their diplomatic approach can help resolve disputes and foster a sense of unity among their peers. However, this can sometimes lead to them avoiding confrontation or suppressing their own needs to keep the peace, so it's important for their friends to encourage open communication. In social settings, Fish friends are often the ones who bring a sense of calm and relaxation.

The Fish Partner

The Fish's emotional sensitivity, intuition, and romantic nature make them loving and devoted partners. They have an innate ability to understand and share the feelings of others, which allows them to be supportive and caring. Their sensitivity, however, can also make them prone to taking on their partner's burdens, so it's essential for the relationship to have a balance where both partners can support each other. Romantic to their core, the Fish brings a dreamy and idealistic approach to love. They are imaginative and creative, often finding unique and beautiful ways to express their affection. Whether through heartfelt messages, spontaneous acts of kindness, or elaborate romantic gestures, a Fish partner will continuously strive to make their partner feel special and valued. Their ability to see the world through a lens of wonder and fantasy can turn everyday moments into magical experiences. Fish tend to idealize their partners and the relationship, sometimes setting unrealistic expectations. When reality does not meet these ideals, they can feel disillusioned or disappointed. Open communication and grounded expectations are crucial in maintaining a healthy balance between their dreams and reality.

Fish partners are also deeply intuitive. They often have a keen sense of their partner's thoughts and feelings, sometimes even before their partner does. This intuition can create a strong emotional bond, as they are able to respond to their partner's needs almost instinctively. However, this heightened sensitivity means they are also vulnerable to being hurt by criticism or conflict. They thrive in relationships where there is mutual respect, understanding, and emotional security. Support and encouragement from their partner are vital for a Fish to feel secure and valued. They are highly adaptable in relationships and willing to make sacrifices for the sake of their loved one's happiness. This selflessness is a beautiful trait, but it's important for their partners to ensure that Fish do not lose themselves in the relationship. Encouraging their individuality and supporting their personal dreams and aspirations can help maintain a healthy dynamic.

A relationship with a Fish partner is characterized by deep emotional connection, empathy, and romanticism. They are intuitive, compassionate, and incredibly loving, making them devoted and attentive partners. While their idealistic nature can sometimes lead to challenges, with open communication and mutual support, a relationship with a Fish can be profoundly fulfilling and spiritually enriching.

SWALLOW

☆ ☆ ☆

January 15–February 7

Swallows have tremendous potential, although they are often too self-conscious of their failures and ignore their achievements. They also tend to withdraw when in difficulty, occupying themselves with a chosen pursuit that isolates them. Although graceful in the air, the swallow is a vulnerable bird on land. Similarly, those born in the Swallow sign are more artistic than technical and not at their best when concentrating on materialistic pursuits, which are best left to others. Just as the swallow is seldom seen to land, a prime trait of those born in this cycle is reticence and hesitation regarding down-to-earth, practical concerns. Overcoming inertia is their primary obstacle, but they can achieve remarkable results quickly once they overcome this initial hurdle.

Swallows are true romantics and love to fantasize and reminisce. Many share a marvelous talent for captivating an audience, enlivening conversation with sheer enthusiasm for romance and adventure. The phrase "still waters run deep" is often an apt description of the Swallow. Indeed, many give the impression that somewhere within their soul lies a myriad of secrets. Swallows are natural performers, and a flamboyant, dramatic personality never fails to win friends and gain influence. They enjoy a variety of interests, and few will remain in the same job or social circumstances for their entire lives. Swallows seldom do anything in a conventional style but lend a showy, theatrical quality to their manifold ventures.

It is vital for Swallows to feel good about themselves. They will devote much time to their appearance and care greatly for their health and fitness.

Those born in this sign hate to be disturbed when unprepared and prefer friends and relatives to let them know when they intend to visit. The Swallow will frequently display an unorthodox attitude toward life and live according to their own rules and values. The Swallow is always prepared to help those in distress. They are gracious and generous, excellent listeners, and amiable friends. However, they cannot abide gossip and refuse to continue with a conversation that turns into criticism of anyone not present. They love company and make great hosts.

Swallows tend to be elegant dressers, although they are not blind followers of fashion. In their opinion, if it is not the latest trend—so what! Swallows are neat, although they are often forgetful and constantly mislaying possessions.

The Swallow will not seek to be the center of attention. If pressed, however, they will rise to any occasion. They refuse to be bored and are always searching for new ideas. Once anything becomes routine, they look for something else to add to their list of interests. Sometimes, they fail to acknowledge their abilities, lacking faith in their talents and potential. Swallows often start a job at home, such as painting, decorating, or fixing the car, only to leave it unfinished. You can always tell the Swallow house by a half-mown lawn or an abandoned piece of home improvement. Nevertheless, the houses of those born in this cycle are particularly clean and tidy, and their gardens neat and well-tended.

The Swallow likes to be surrounded by love and fellowship. They make excellent family people, and so long as they have a secure environment to return to each evening, they will excel in their chosen profession. They will work confidently with business colleagues, knowing precisely what they want and how to achieve it. Their strength of purpose comes from the knowledge that they are working for the benefit of their family.

Swallows are renowned for their forward-thinking and expansive vision, both for their personal growth and the advancement of the world. They are deeply committed to progressive ideals and are dedicated to instigating positive transformations in the world. Those born in this sign are often at the forefront of humanitarian efforts, whether contributing to the fight against environmental degradation, advocating for solutions to global hunger, or championing social justice causes. With a firm adherence to their principles, Swallows are unwavering in their determination to create a better world. Their actions are guided by a profound sense of compassion and a fervent belief in fairness. Additionally, the Swallow prioritizes freedom and is passionate about ensuring it for everyone. People born in the Swallow sign are often at the forefront when it comes to ushering in transformative change.

Positive Characteristics

A cheerful temperament makes most relationships easy for Swallows, and many enjoy considerable popularity. Love of social occasions is usual, with much concern for the pleasure and happiness of others. Business capacity is well above average, although partners or colleagues are required to help with sound administration and investments. Most born in this sign have a deep sense of responsibility, generally sharing a conscientious and principled attitude to life. Swallows are dedicated workers who can devote themselves long and hard to positive effect. With their exceptional intelligence and cerebral nature, Swallow individuals are known for their intellectual curiosity. They delve deep into thought, analyzing various situational aspects when seeking solutions. Their unique ability to perceive potential in everything and their pleasure in thorough examination make them tolerant of diverse viewpoints. Swallows are renowned for their big-picture thinking and are often regarded as some of the best problem-solvers. While they may become preoccupied with their thoughts, they are excellent people to approach when seeking impartial and informed advice. Swallows are known for their charm, diplomacy, and balanced nature. They are highly social and value harmonious relationships, often acting as peacemakers in conflicts. They possess a keen sense of fairness and justice, striving for equality in their interactions. Their creativity and appreciation for beauty often lead them to artistic pursuits. They are gracious, open-minded, and adaptable, making them excellent collaborators. Swallows strongly desire to understand different perspectives, enhancing their empathy and understanding. Their optimism and positive outlook on life attract many friends and admirers.

Negative Characteristics

Many Swallows miss vital opportunities due to procrastination resulting from a hesitant and indecisive attitude and a desire to weigh all options. Until proved right or successful, Swallows show a lack of confidence and too much dependence on the opinions of others. Extravagance and a love of luxury can create financial problems. Sometimes, Swallows have unrealistic ideals or aspirations, and disappointments are bound to result. There is the risk that Swallows will withdraw, becoming silent or self-pitying when difficulties arise. There is also a tendency for Swallows to be possessive in relationships. Swallows are inclined toward deep thinking, which can sometimes result in condescension. They often firmly believe that their thoughts are always right, leading them to view others as wrong. Typically, the Swallow is oblivious that they may come across as talking down to others because they genuinely consider their opinions undeniable truths. Once a Swallow forms an opinion, it can be challenging to sway them from it. This tendency can cause frustration for individuals attempting to suggest solutions or engage in discussions with those born in this sign, leaving them feeling intellectually inferior and unequal. Swallows might avoid confrontation, sometimes resulting in passive-aggressiveness. Their need for harmony can make them people-pleasers, compromising their own needs to keep others happy. They can be overly concerned with appearances, valuing superficial qualities over substance. Additionally, Swallows may struggle with inconsistency, wavering between extremes. Their tendency to seek approval can lead to insecurity and dependence on others for validation.

❋ Appearance

Those born in the sign of the Swallow usually have long and graceful limbs. Endowed with a fine bone structure, the face of the Swallow is warm and sensual. Their eyes are bright, alert, and expressive, often with prominent lashes. They are alert and elegant. Their dress sense can be immaculate, and many Swallows will spend considerable time and effort making sure they look their best. Those born in this sign tend to dress in a way that makes them stand out. They generally move slowly and deliberately, and when at rest, they can remain quiet and still for long periods. Few Swallows are fidgeters or appear nervous. Swallows often exude a refined and graceful appearance, characterized by balanced facial features and a harmonious look. They typically have well-proportioned bodies and an elegant demeanor. Common traits include clear skin, expressive, often almond-shaped eyes, and a warm and welcoming smile. Their hair is usually well-kept and often styled to complement their overall look. Swallows have a keen sense of fashion, favoring elegant and tasteful clothing that highlights their natural charm. Their posture is upright and poised, reflecting their inner balance and confidence. Overall, they project an aura of beauty and sophistication.

❋ Health

The throat and larynx are the primary areas of susceptibility to infection in the body. Swallows, known for their tendency to internalize their feelings, often experience stress-related issues. Despite their outward appearance of calm and composure, Swallows frequently struggle with internalized problems. Stiff joints are a commonly reported ailment among Swallows, although regular exercise generally alleviates discomfort. While many Swallows boast a robust metabolism, their dietary choices can lead to weight-related challenges. Swallows typically enjoy good health, often maintaining balance through a healthy lifestyle.

However, they might experience issues related to the kidneys and lower back. Stress management and maintaining harmony in relationships are crucial for their overall well-being.

The Formula for Success

The Swallow is an invaluable asset to any group or team, always willing to lend a helping hand to their peers. They consistently bring innovative ideas to the table, and their unique approach adds a touch of flair to everything they do. Known for their compassion and flexibility, Swallows are always willing to set a positive example for others. They are averse to conflict and will go to great lengths to avoid unnecessary disputes, prioritizing the happiness and well-being of those around them. However, they are quick to defend their friends and can eloquently advocate on their behalf when necessary. Swallows are open-minded and fair, always willing to consider the perspectives of others without bias. Their vibrant imaginations, artistic abilities, and creative talents are used for the betterment of the community. Additionally, Swallows feel a deep connection to nature and possess a strong spiritual side. Their empathy drives them to seek out and alleviate suffering wherever it may be found.

Words of Advice

The practicalities of life do not always align with the Swallow's imaginative aspirations. Many have unrealistic attitudes toward material pursuits and often experience disappointment due to high expectations. They display humility and are seldom, if ever, arrogant or vain. While these qualities are admirable, they may lead to too much self-sacrifice and a lack of consideration for their personal needs. Swallows should make a determined effort not to let acquaintances walk all over them. Those born under this sign are sometimes too kind and generous for their own good. Like the high-flying swallow bird, people born during this zodiac sign tend to be somewhat aloof, and there is a tendency for them to appear to look down on others. Swallows should try harder to make others feel at ease when pointing out faults by adding compliments and praise to their criticism.

❋ Suitable Occupations

The compassionate and empathetic Swallow is well suited to working with marginalized communities, individuals in ill health, and the elderly. Their caring nature and ability to actively listen make them excellent candidates for counseling, therapy, and social work roles. Swallows possess strong communication skills, making them well suited for professions that involve persuasion and direct customer interaction. Additionally, their affinity for nature makes many Swallows well suited for agriculture, conservation, and animal welfare careers. Furthermore, their natural inclination toward the dramatic arts often leads Swallows to excel in careers related to music and drama. Swallows are known for their diplomacy, charm, and sense of justice, making them well suited for various occupations. Their natural ability to mediate and find balance in conflicts makes them excellent candidates for careers as lawyers, judges, or mediators. Their strong sense of fairness and ethical standards align well with these roles, where they can advocate for justice and equality. Swallows' social skills and love for interacting with others make them great fits for public relations and human resources. They can manage relationships effectively, ensuring smooth communication and harmony within organizations. Their creativity and appreciation for beauty make them ideal for careers in the arts, including roles as designers, artists, or fashion consultants. They have an eye for aesthetics and can excel in creating visually pleasing works. Additionally, Swallows' strong communication skills and persuasiveness are assets in marketing, sales, and diplomacy careers. They can present ideas compellingly and build strong connections with clients and stakeholders. Swallows' ability to create pleasant and harmonious environments shines in hospitality and event planning, making guests feel welcomed and satisfied. Overall, Swallows thrive in careers that allow them to use their creativity and sense of fairness, contributing to environments that value balance and harmony.

The Swallow at Work

The Swallow personality type is characterized by an amiable and popular nature in the workplace. Swallows are known for their trustworthiness and reliability in keeping confidence. They excel as sympathetic listeners and are always ready to support their colleagues. However, they may not always be the best at diplomatic communication, often providing advice others may not be prepared to hear. Swallows thrive as dedicated and dependable workers, preferring to work independently and shining when given the freedom to do so. They are ambitious individuals who work diligently to achieve their goals. However, Swallows may struggle under pressure, often flustered and forgetful when stressed. They excel in roles requiring quick thinking, adaptability, and collaboration. Swallows are natural team players, often bringing people together with their excellent communication skills and positive energy. They are resourceful problem-solvers who navigate challenges and find innovative solutions swiftly. Their enthusiasm and versatility make them valuable assets in the fast-paced media, marketing, and technology industries. However, their preference for variety can make them restless in monotonous tasks. They are able to maximize their potential and thrive in roles that offer diversity, creative freedom, and growth opportunities.

The Swallow Parent

Swallow parents are patient, tolerant, and strongly averse to punishment or severe reprimand. They believe in allowing their offspring to make mistakes, considering them valuable learning experiences. They are affectionate and loving, providing their young with guidance and support. While they prefer their children to be clean and tidy, they do not express anger if their offspring return home dirty or muddy from playing. Innovative and creative, Swallow parents constantly come up with unconventional ideas for entertaining and educating their young through creative projects. They are enthusiastic about involving their children in extracurricular activities, particularly in the arts, rather than sports or science. This nurturing and supportive approach reflects

Swallow parents' unique and caring nature, creating a positive and enriching environment for their offspring.

The Swallow Child

The Swallow is known for being a lively, curious, and imaginative child. They often have an active imagination and may even have invisible friends. Swallow children tend to talk to themselves more frequently than other signs, but they are also sociable and easily make friends with other children. Their vivid imagination allows them to create rich and colorful worlds of make-believe. They are quick learners from a young age, although they may need encouragement to excel in school. When presented with stimulating and interesting subject matter, Swallow children enthusiastically approach learning. Teachers may need to work hard to capture the Swallow child's attention by making lessons particularly engaging. A Swallow child, embodying agility and curiosity, is energetic and eager to explore the world. They are quick learners who adapt easily to new situations and thrive in dynamic environments. Their inquisitiveness drives them to ask questions and seek knowledge, making them enthusiastic students. However, their boundless energy and desire for variety can lead to restlessness. Encouraging their interests and providing diverse activities helps channel their energy positively, fostering their growth and creativity.

The Swallow Friend

Swallows are special friends, good listeners, and entertaining conversationalists, but they must share a common bond or affinity to enjoy close friendships. They are easygoing and hate to burden anyone with their troubles. Although Swallows are quick to offer advice and can be openly critical of others, it is not done in malice. Generally, they refuse to judge their acquaintances, maintaining an open mind in most situations. Swallows sometimes seem to exist in an insular, timeless world. They are always late for appointments, hate to be hurried, and insist on doing everything in their own good time. Swallows tend to talk to themselves when working, thinking, or preparing. They are also garrulous in conversation, forever going off on tangents from the topic being discussed. Strangely enough, this can create a sense of shared reverie, a remarkably calming influence on those who are anxious, worried, or under stress. One always feels that everything will work out for the best after a chat with a Swallow friend.

The Swallow Partner

Individuals born under the Swallow sign are often characterized by their calm and serene demeanor, which enables them to effectively navigate relationships with partners who may be more high-strung or intense. Their presence has a soothing and tranquilizing effect on those around them. Swallows are not inclined to thrive in environments that prioritize constant activity and excitement. They prefer to observe, absorb, and contribute thoughtful insights at their own pace rather than be swept up in relentless enthusiasm. The Swallow partner is romantic and affectionate, often wearing their heart on their sleeve. They tend to be a little sentimental, but this just adds to their charm. They are open and giving, often trusting others too easily. However, they are also drawn to those who bring excitement and adventure into their lives if it doesn't disrupt their sense of stability.

For the Swallow to thrive in a relationship, they require a partner who is responsible and provides a sense of stability. However, their partner must also share their imaginative and creative spirit for the relationship to truly flourish. Individuals who lack sensitivity and understanding are generally unattractive to those born under the Swallow sign. Swallows are often recognized for their ambitious vision and forward-thinking nature. They are driven by a deep-rooted sense of justice and an unwavering desire to bring about positive change in the world. Their humanitarian endeavors frequently involve addressing pressing global issues such as climate change and world hunger. While they can be resolute in their convictions, they are committed to improving the world and cherish the concept of freedom for all individuals. As such they can make the very best and most stimulating partners.

EAGLE

★ ★ ★

February 8–March 1

In ancient Mesopotamian mythology, the celestial Eagle was revered as a symbol of strength, courage, and a daring spirit. Those born under this sign are known for their practical and intuitive nature. They possess a remarkable ability to approach challenges comprehensively and are adept at finding solutions. Individuals born under this sign also have a special gift for understanding and empathizing with others, making them perceptive and compassionate.

People born in this sign often have captivating and attentive personalities. They tend to have a calm and composed exterior but are deeply emotional individuals underneath that facade. They are driven by a strong sense of purpose and possess an innate understanding of fairness and morality. One of their remarkable traits is their readiness to acknowledge and rectify their mistakes. They are unafraid to adapt their viewpoints and approaches, demonstrating a genuine willingness to grow and evolve. They highly value constructive criticism, as they find it essential to personal development. They frequently seek input from their friends and peers in various situations, valuing different perspectives and insights.

Eagles possess exceptional skills in assessing circumstances impartially. They avoid taking sides during conflicts and approach situations fairly and without bias. These admirable qualities enable Eagles to develop comprehensive plans and make rational decisions. Before acting, the Eagle carefully observes, listens, and absorbs information, demonstrating a thoughtful and deliberate approach to conflict resolution. Despite their personal beliefs, Eagles strive to acknowledge and appreciate the validity of all viewpoints, indicating their open-mindedness and willingness to consider different perspectives. Eagles are ever receptive to persuasion, especially when presented with solid reasoning and evidence.

Individuals born under the sign of Eagle are socially adaptable and excel in intellectual conversations. They are deeply committed to their unconventional beliefs and can transition from enthusiastic conversationalists to contemplative thinkers in moments. Despite forming meaningful connections, they may come across as distant at times. It's essential for those who know Eagle to embrace and appreciate them for who they are.

People born under this sign are often attracted to individuals who lead exciting or unconventional lives, as they highly value these traits in their social circle. Ideally, their friends and romantic partners should also embrace an unconventional approach to life. Eagles often adopt an unconventional style. Even those who are dedicated fashion followers or must dress formally for work will always make an individual statement in their chosen attire.

In romantic relationships, those born under this sign are considerate and giving, but they strongly emphasize the need for personal space. They dislike feeling like others intrude on their private thoughts and reflections. Mental privacy is paramount to the Eagle, who will passionately defend it. By contrast, those born in this sign are fascinated by the intentions and motivations of others, be they friends, lovers, or mere acquaintances. They are determined to discover just what it is that makes people tick. The Eagle, therefore, has a paradoxical, enigmatic personality that others can find enchanting. While they may seem to keep to themselves, they rarely have secrets; rather, they require moments of solitude. This mental isolation often enables them to find solutions to their problems and those of others. They approach everything as a task to be accomplished, making them independent and diligent. With a clear objective and a well-thought-out plan, they can achieve anything they set their minds to, regardless of the level of effort required. They hold themselves and others to high standards and tend to be more conservative than some zodiac signs.

Individuals born during the Eagle sign are characterized by their unwavering determination and strong work ethic. They display remarkable persistence across all aspects of their lives, whether in their professional endeavors, personal passions, or duties at home. Their steadfast commitment often leads to success, making them exceptionally well suited for entrepreneurial ventures. Eagle individuals eagerly seize opportunities to expand their skills and wholeheartedly devote themselves to achieving their goals, always holding their own resolute determination and hard work in high regard.

An Eagle, symbolizing strength and vision, possesses a commanding and ambitious character. They are natural leaders, driven by a desire to achieve and excel. With sharp intellect and keen insight, they easily identify opportunities and strategize effectively. Eagles are confident and determined, facing challenges head-on and inspiring others with resilience. Their high standards and focus can sometimes come off as intense, but their loyalty and integrity earn them deep respect. Independent yet deeply principled, Eagles thrive when pursuing goals that align with their strong sense of purpose and justice. Their visionary nature makes them exceptional pioneers and innovators.

Positive Characteristics

Eagles are known for their energetic, engaging, and vibrant personalities. They often find themselves in the spotlight due to their dramatic flair and flamboyant nature and exude confidence in most situations. Their unique ability to see the bigger picture, mystical inclination, and well-developed intuition draw many of them to philosophical and spiritual pursuits. With their creativity, adaptability, and imagination, Eagles are often seen as creative thinkers with many distinctive ideas. Driven by their ambition, Eagles continually set and achieve admirable goals through hard work, determination, and concerted effort. Their constant drive to outperform themselves and others motivates them to overcome difficulties. These qualities ensure that many individuals born under this sign succeed in their professional and leisure endeavors. Whether excelling as exceptional athletes or dominating in the world of online gaming, Eagles thrive with a competitive spirit and determination. The Eagle birth sign symbolizes vision, strength, and leadership. Individuals born during this sign possess a sharp intellect and keen awareness, allowing them to see opportunities and challenges from a higher perspective. They are natural leaders, inspiring and guiding others with confidence and charisma. Their determination and resilience enable them to overcome obstacles and achieve their goals. Eagles are also highly intuitive, often relying on their instincts to make important decisions. Their loyalty and protective nature make them dependable friends and allies. With a strong sense of justice and integrity, they strive to impact the world around them positively.

Negative Characteristics

People born during the sign of Eagle display a remarkable ability to immerse themselves in intricate mental landscapes, often escaping into their imagination when confronted with formidable obstacles. Although their vivid inner world allows them to dream big, this tendency can sometimes hinder their success in practical matters, leading to dashed hopes from unrealistic expectations. This inclination toward wishful thinking also poses potential risks in business endeavors. Eagles' outspoken nature and unconventional perspectives may attract criticism, as they are not afraid to express their opinions freely. While they excel at managing their households with practicality and skill, their disinterest in financial matters can lead to personal challenges. Eagles throw themselves wholeheartedly into their endeavors, often becoming intensely focused and overly enthusiastic, sometimes to the exclusion of friends, family, and partners. Their pursuit of perfectionism means they view failure as a considerable setback rather than a challenge to conquer or move beyond. When faced with setbacks, their resulting despondency can have a ripple effect on the emotions of those around them.

Appearance

Eagles often possess striking physical characteristics, characterized by their expressive and intense eyes that reflect their thoughtful and determined nature. Despite their swift reflexes, they exhibit deliberate and purposeful movements, projecting an aura of calculated intention with every step. Even during moments of repose, individuals born under this sign are seldom seen slouching or sprawled out; instead they maintain a poised and upright posture. Their naturally slender physique and distinctive facial features contribute to their unwavering and authoritative demeanor. From their deep and resolute gazes to their prominent cheekbones and defined browbones, individuals born under this sign exude a sense of determination and strength.

Health

Eagle individuals are known for their remarkable dedication and perseverance in pursuing their goals and aspirations. This steadfast commitment may sometimes lead to feelings of stress and anxiety. Still, they excel in managing their lives to minimize the likelihood of experiencing digestive or stomach-related issues. Born under this sign, Eagle individuals exhibit extraordinary resilience, and their bodies have an incredible ability for rapid healing and recovery from injuries. They typically possess strong physical stamina and a resilient constitution, allowing them to tackle life's challenges with vigor. Their active lifestyle and love for the outdoors keep them fit and energetic. However, their intense drive and ambition can lead to stress-related issues if not managed properly. Eagles must balance their high-energy pursuits with relaxation and mindfulness practices. Maintaining a balanced diet and regular exercise routine supports their overall well-being. Preventive care and stress management are essential for keeping an Eagle in peak health and ready to soar.

The Formula for Success

Eagles are known for their strong moral compass and commitment to truth, sincerity, and idealism. Their decision-making is a blend of logical reasoning and intuitive insight, which positions them well for success in various pursuits. They are renowned for their industrious nature, keen intellect, and adeptness at communicating clearly and persuasively.

In social settings, they are affable, easygoing with acquaintances, undemanding as friends, and supportive as colleagues. Eagles possess a remarkable capacity for imaginative thinking and a rare ability to empathize and understand diverse perspectives. They meticulously analyze all facets of a problem before arriving at conclusions, often producing innovative and revolutionary ideas. Known for their unparalleled creativity and a treasury of original concepts, Eagles are remarkably flexible and have a vibrant imagination. They are marked by unyielding ambition and a propensity for setting and attaining commendable goals through unwavering determination. The Eagle formula for success hinges on balance, diplomacy, and collaboration. Eagles thrive by creating harmony in their environments, ensuring equitable and fair outcomes. By leveraging their innate charm and social intelligence, Eagles can influence and inspire those around them. They prioritize strategic decision-making and thoughtful planning, balancing logic with intuition. Embracing their artistic flair and appreciation for beauty, Eagles bring creativity to their pursuits, often finding innovative solutions. Ultimately, their success is built on equilibrium, fairness, and strong interpersonal connections.

Words of Advice

Some individuals born under the Eagle sign are known for their idealistic nature, often finding solace in daydreams and even fantasies when faced with a daunting challenge. This inclination toward escapism can lead them to become introverted, secretive, and emotionally distant as they seek to evade the harsh realities of life. Eagles must acknowledge and confront these tendencies, understanding that life does not always unfold as expected. Additionally, Eagles may find themselves deeply engrossed in their work, often to the point of excess. When they believe in a cause, they wholeheartedly dedicate themselves to it, sometimes at the cost of neglecting their relationships, family life, and daily responsibilities. Recognizing and addressing this deeply committed yet potentially obsessive aspect of their character is vital for the well-being of Eagles.

Suitable Occupations

Individuals born under the sign of Eagle often possess a natural inclination toward seeking the spotlight and demonstrate exceptional skills in public speaking, performing arts, and endeavors requiring the art of persuasion. Many accomplished advertising professionals and sales executives born under this sign are adept at leveraging their innate charm and proficient communication skills to succeed in their respective careers. Moreover, their practical and analytical inclinations make them well suited for roles in engineering and technology, enabling them to effectively utilize their problem-solving capabilities and innovative mindset to develop and improve complex systems and products. Their unwavering dedication also makes them well-equipped for computer science and information technology careers, as they excel in tasks that demand precision and meticulous attention to detail. Those born during this astrological sign possess an unquenchable thirst for knowledge, which drives them to pursue academic interests and expand their understanding of the world. Their bold and inquisitive nature makes them well suited for scientific research, where they can challenge existing boundaries and contribute to humanity's collective knowledge. Moreover, their sharp attention to detail and profound admiration for beauty inspire them to harness their creativity across various artistic mediums, including photography, painting, sculpture, architecture, and commercial art. Their exceptional artistic talents and meticulous approach empower them to thrive and leave a lasting impression in these creative domains.

The Eagle at Work

Individuals born under the Eagle sign are known for their remarkable ability to adapt to various work situations and flexibility in handling tasks. They possess a deep understanding of people and are known for their empathetic nature, making them exceptionally well suited for leadership roles. An Eagle employer embodies traits such as a strong sense of fairness, an unwavering work ethic, and the ability to set a positive example for others. Eagle employees excel in fostering positive and harmonious relationships with their peers. They have a natural talent for mediating conflicts and resolving issues with fairness and justice. For Eagle individuals, the ideal profession involves challenges and opportunities to take on leadership roles. They thrive in environments that provide stimulation and avenues for creative expression. Without these elements, individuals born under the Eagle sign are unlikely to find lasting contentment in their work.

The Eagle Parent

Ambitious Eagle parents set high standards for themselves and their children, and they inspire their families to strive for excellence. With keen insight and strategic thinking, Eagle parents are adept at guiding their children through challenges, providing clear direction and support. They are fiercely loyal and deeply committed, ensuring their family feels secure and well cared for. Their strong sense of justice and fairness translates into a parenting style emphasizing integrity and responsibility. Eagle parents encourage independence and resilience in their children, fostering an environment where individuality and ambition are celebrated. However, their high expectations can sometimes be intense, so Eagle parents must balance their drive with patience and understanding. By nurturing their children's unique strengths and providing a balanced mix of guidance and freedom, Eagle parents cultivate a harmonious and thriving family dynamic.

The Eagle Child

An Eagle child, embodying the traits of strength and vision, is naturally confident and ambitious from a young age. They exhibit a strong sense of independence and determination, often setting high goals for themselves and striving to achieve them. These children are intellectually curious with a keen desire to understand the world around them, making them quick learners and enthusiastic students. Eagle children are natural leaders, often taking charge in group settings and inspiring their peers with their vision and decisiveness. They have a strong sense of justice and fairness, which drives them to stand up for what they believe is right. However, their intense drive can sometimes lead to frustration if things don't go their way. Teaching them patience and the value of perseverance is crucial. They thrive in environments that challenge them mentally and physically, and they benefit greatly from opportunities to explore and develop their leadership skills. Encouraging a balance between striving to meet their ambitions and having enough downtime is key to nurturing their well-rounded growth.

The Eagle Friend

Individuals under this sign strive to establish a distinctive and influential presence within their social groups. Eagles steer clear of dogmatic, inflexible, or stagnant individuals and strongly oppose prejudice and injustice. Eagles often find it challenging to develop lasting friendships due to their captivating and charismatic nature, simultaneously presenting unique perspectives and preferences that may not align with typical social activities. Nonetheless, when they meet someone who shares their values and beliefs, Eagles excel at captivating their newfound companion, drawing them into a world of wonder and adventure. Friends of those born during the Eagle birth sign enjoy a loyal, supportive, and inspiring companion. Eagle friends defend and support their loved ones. They possess a keen intuition, often understanding their friends' needs and feelings without words. Their natural leadership and vision inspire those around them, encouraging personal growth and ambition. Eagles value honesty and integrity, making them trustworthy and dependable confidants. Their adventurous spirit ensures that friendships are filled with excitement and memorable experiences.

The Eagle Partner

An Eagle partner possesses a robust and resilient nature. They are not easily deterred by challenges and approach obstacles with determination and confidence. This strength provides a solid foundation for the relationship, ensuring stability and security. They are the rock in times of trouble, offering unwavering support and guidance. Eagles are natural visionaries. They have a clear sense of direction and purpose in their personal and professional lives. This ambitious streak means they constantly strive for excellence and encourage their partner to reach their highest potential. They set lofty goals for the relationship, always looking toward a brighter future and ensuring their partner feels motivated and inspired. They are decisive and proactive, preferring to take the initiative in planning and decision-making. Their partner can rely on them to steer the relationship through various phases confidently and clearly. However, this strong leadership is balanced with a deep sense of fairness and respect for their partner's opinions and needs.

An Eagle partner is protective and caring, always looking for their partner's well-being. They are attentive to their partner's needs and are quick to offer support and comfort. Their nurturing side ensures that their partner feels loved and valued, reinforcing the emotional security of the relationship. While an Eagle partner's high standards and ambitious nature can be motivating, it can also lead to high expectations that may sometimes feel overwhelming. Eagle partners must practice patience and empathy, recognizing that not everyone moves at their pace or shares their drive level. Encouraging open dialogue about these differences can help mitigate potential conflicts and ensure both partners feel heard and appreciated. Eagles value their independence and respect their partner's need for personal space and individuality. They understand the importance of balancing time together with time apart, allowing each partner to grow individually while still nurturing the relationship.

FOX

★ ★ ★

March 2–March 20

In Mesopotamian tradition, the fox symbolized resilience. People born under this sign are remarkably willing to take risks and pursue new ventures without hesitation. When their risks pay off, they have the potential to achieve extraordinary success. Despite facing ridicule and criticism from others, those born under this sign persist in their beliefs and remain unwavering in their determination to achieve their goals. Fearless and unafraid to speak their mind, Foxes offer authentic and truthful feedback. Their outspoken nature, a powerful expression of their authenticity, is not driven by malice; they are straightforward and eager to express their thoughts.

The individuals represented by the Fox sign possess a unique ability to gracefully adapt to new and unexpected situations. Their innate strength lies in their remarkable versatility and capacity to handle various challenges. This adaptability, while sometimes causing them to overlook pitfalls others might notice, inspires them. Those born under this sign radiate with confidence and are at their best when conquering problems and facing obstacles head-on. They are known for their kindness, thoughtfulness, and highly energetic nature. Their driving force is the desire to adapt to current circumstances and create new opportunities from few resources. This exceptional ability allows them to achieve successes others may not consider possible. It's important to note that while they excel at adeptly maneuvering around obstacles, the

Fox may encounter difficulties when attempting to restart and recover after things go awry.

Foxes tend to prioritize their actions and commitments over their appearance, often putting less emphasis on fashion. They may struggle with their fashion sense but are always willing to dress appropriately for different occasions, even if it means adhering to a specific dress code at work, sometimes making them appear somewhat uncomfortable. Despite this, they generally appear neat and can exude a certain relaxed confidence when sporting a casual look. Their discerning taste in music is often evident, although they don't usually make the best dancers. Foxes are adept at socializing but tend to have a small circle of friends. They are fiercely protective of their friends and readily stand up for them in the face of overbearing, controlling, or aggressive individuals.

People born under the Fox sign are known for their unconventional and unique approach to life. They are recognized for their creativity, cleverness, and deep knowledge of various subjects. Their straightforwardness and tendency to express their thoughts without considering others' perceptions often make them stand out. Many people are attracted to Foxes' non-traditional way of living and can appreciate their eccentricities. Despite being adventurous, Foxes may struggle in leadership roles because they assume that others are as capable as they are, sometimes overlooking that others may need support. Additionally, individuals born under this sign may have difficulty being attentive listeners, often distracted by their phones or other thoughts when others are talking.

People born under the zodiac sign of the Fox may not excel in financial management. They forget to pay bills on time and often pursue credit opportunities beyond their means. They are known for taking risks and sometimes enjoy gambling, so it's wise for them to carefully consider any get-rich-quick schemes before committing. As Foxes may incline toward extravagance, it's often recommended that they hand over money matters to others. Despite this, they usually experience good fortune, and their risks frequently pay off. They are naturally generous but may find that money tends to slip through their fingers. People born during this sign are characterized by their courage and determination, often taking on the roles of trailblazers, embracing exploration with a fearless spirit and a willingness to enter uncharted territories. Their boldness and fearlessness make them well suited for embracing significant risks, seeking new experiences, and pioneering fresh paths. They are typically optimistic, unburdened by concerns of the past, and filled with hope and exuberance. They possess a striking combination of generosity and humor, displaying a unique and enjoyable sense of wit.

Positive Characteristics

The Fox is known for constantly generating new and innovative conceptual ideas, drawing from a deep well of resourcefulness and imagination. Those born under this sign possess a unique blend of artistic and technical talents, enabling them to bring their visions to life in remarkable ways. Always seeking novelty and unafraid to take bold risks, the Fox approaches life with a sense of adventure and unwavering optimism. They are not easily swayed from their pursuits and maintain a positive outlook, even when facing challenges. With an emotional and romantic disposition, individuals born under the Fox sign often demonstrate a strong concern for those around them. They are thoughtful and reliable, known for their deep sense of loyalty to both their ideals and the people they care about. Obstacles are seen as opportunities for growth, and Foxes refuse to let anything hinder their vibrant and stimulating way of life. Lively and passionate, those born in this sign possess a dynamic and adventurous spirit that fuels their creative, energetic, and courageous pursuits. Their positive mindset is contagious, uplifting those around them and inspiring others to embrace life with the same zest and determination. The Fox birth sign symbolizes intelligence, adaptability, and charm. They are quick-witted and resourceful, easily navigating complex situations creatively. Their adaptability allows them to thrive in diverse environments, making them excellent problem-solvers. Fox individuals are also known for their charismatic and persuasive nature, effortlessly attracting and inspiring those around them. They possess a keen intuition, often sensing opportunities and potential pitfalls before others.

This sign's playful and curious spirit drives their love for adventure and exploration, ensuring they live vibrant, fulfilling lives. Loyal and protective, Fox individuals are dedicated friends and partners.

Negative Characteristics

Foxes often face challenges in achieving their aspirations due to an unrealistic outlook on life. Their tendency to ignore problems and overlook potential risks can lead to complications. Individuals born under this sign are known for their strong-willed and sometimes stubborn nature, which can lead to conflicts with authority figures and difficulties in family relationships. They are inclined to extravagance and may make errors in managing their finances and investments. While they are open to taking bold risks, they may struggle to bounce back from setbacks. Foxes tend to commit to their pursuits wholeheartedly and have a habit of being forgetful and misplacing items due to their creative and inventive inclinations. They also tend to become absorbed in their thoughts, often leading them to disregard advice or input from others. The Fox, while gifted with many strengths, also has their share of challenges. Individuals born under this sign can be overly cunning and manipulative, using their intelligence for personal gain at the expense of others. Their adaptability may lead to a lack of stability and consistency, making them seem unreliable or unpredictable. Fox individuals can be overly curious, often meddling in affairs that don't concern them, leading to conflicts and misunderstandings. Their charm, while usually a strength, can become deceitful, masking their true intentions. Additionally, their strong desire for independence can make them distant and aloof in relationships.

Appearance

People born under the sign of the Fox are characterized by their lively and expressive way of communicating. They are known for using exaggerated gestures with their long and graceful arms. Regarding clothing, they prioritize comfort over style and are not particularly concerned with neatness unless necessary. These individuals are talkative and animated, often becoming the center of attention at social gatherings due to their dynamic presence. While they can be deeply engrossed in a topic that catches their interest, they are not shy about showing disinterest if they become bored.

Health

People born under this astrological sign frequently struggle with sleeplessness, finding it difficult to attain a peaceful and uninterrupted rest, which leads to restless nights. This issue becomes more pronounced when they are deeply engrossed in activities that fully capture their attention. Prolonged periods of stress and deep focus can lead to headaches or migraines. Furthermore, challenges may trigger feelings of sadness or even depression in individuals born in this sign. Their daring nature also makes them more susceptible to experiencing a greater number of injuries.

The Formula for Success

People born in the Fox sign are known for their multifaceted perspective, deep understanding of their tasks, and wide range of skills and knowledge. They often prefer being involved in various project aspects rather than specializing in one area. Despite their diverse capabilities, Foxes strive for excellence in their work and are willing to take calculated risks to succeed. They are characterized by their pioneering spirit and unwavering commitment to their endeavors. Foxes are highly imaginative and forward-thinking individuals who thrive in solitary work settings. However, their tendency to take charge may not always translate into effective leadership. For individuals born during the Fox birth sign, the formula for success lies in leveraging their natural intelligence, adaptability, and charm while maintaining integrity and focus. They should channel their quick-wittedness and resourcefulness toward innovative solutions and creative endeavors. Embracing adaptability will allow them to thrive in diverse environments and overcome obstacles.

Cultivating genuine relationships and using their charismatic nature to inspire and lead others is crucial. Foxes should balance their curiosity with discretion, ensuring they respect boundaries. By staying true to their values and fostering loyalty, they can build a strong support network, paving the way for lasting success.

Words of Advice

Those born under the sign of the Fox are often known for their exceptional creativity and a proclivity for generating unconventional and original ideas. Their unique trait is a double-edged sword, as it can draw criticism from those who lack imagination, but it also sets them apart. Foxes are characterized by their willingness to embrace challenges and stand up for their beliefs. They tend to be outspoken about their feelings and convictions, often leading to unnecessary conflicts. It is recommended that individuals born under this sign work on exercising more restraint and make a conscious effort to impress and flatter others, particularly when seeking assistance. Foxes should understand that their present actions hold more significance than past events and recognize their inclination to seek change and variety. However, this mindset could potentially lead to avoiding responsibilities and severing important ties in the future. It's essential for Foxes to refrain from permanently breaking ties with individuals who could be of future help. It's always beneficial to keep doors open for potential support down the line.

Suitable Occupations

Individuals born under this zodiac sign are known for their fearless and adventurous nature, thriving in high-stakes and challenging environments. They are naturally drawn to careers that involve significant risks, such as firefighting, law enforcement, and rescue. Their deep-seated desire to put their lives on the line to assist those in need is a driving force in their career choices. With their excellent communication skills and charismatic manner, they are well suited for political careers, where they passionately advocate for their beliefs and strive to make a positive impact. This zodiac sign's individuals also possess remarkable artistic and musical talents, using their creativity to convey meaningful messages and connect with others profoundly. However, when placed in managerial or leadership roles, they may face challenges as they often try to take charge of everything, not letting others play their part. Their natural inclination to lead may occasionally make it difficult for them to provide their subordinates with the necessary support and encouragement.

The Fox at Work

The persistent Fox excels as a negotiator, particularly in long and difficult bargaining situations. Those who think they can outwit Foxes in a deal are mistaken. Foxes go to great lengths to achieve their goals, often displaying unparalleled determination and tenacity. Many Foxes are self-made individuals with a unique and unorthodox style that sets them apart in any negotiation. However, their strong emotions can drive them forward, sometimes making it challenging for others to keep up with their pace. Foxes often have unconventional and idiosyncratic personalities, with colleagues either admiring them for their bold approach or finding them challenging to work with. There is rarely a middle ground with a Fox; they evoke strong reactions. They can be great allies due to their unwavering commitment, but they can also be formidable adversaries due to their steadfast pursuit of their objectives. Successful working relationships often hinge on maintaining a positive rapport with a Fox, as they value loyalty and respect.

The Fox Parent

Fox parents are known for their nurturing and supportive approach to parenting. They prioritize fostering independence and socialization in their children, aiming to build strong, friendly relationships with them. As their offspring mature, many Fox children maintain close, enjoyable bonds with their parents. Notably, Fox parents eagerly anticipate school breaks as opportunities to plan and engage in enriching activities with their children, creating cherished memories. Despite their high aspirations, Fox parents refrain from burdening their young ones with unrealistic expectations, valuing their children's well-being above all else. Fox parents are cunning and resourceful, always finding creative solutions to problems. They fiercely protect their children, using their sharp instincts to navigate life's challenges. Known for their adaptability, Fox parents can quickly change tactics to support their family best. They value independence and encourage their children to be self-reliant and curious. Playful and clever, Fox parents foster an environment of learning and exploration. They are also highly observant, picking up on subtle cues to understand their children's needs and emotions, ensuring they provide the right guidance and support.

The Fox Child

The Fox child is recognized for their strong-willed and rebellious nature, often defying authority figures such as teachers and parents from an early age. Simply stating something to a Fox child is not sufficient; they will always counter with probing questions. Many Fox children are also exceptionally lively, and when combined with their natural curiosity, they can be quite a handful. Nevertheless, these inquisitive children possess immense learning potential, and if their curiosity is nurtured, they can provide a great deal of entertainment. While many children may be untidy, Fox children often exhibit an exceptional level of disorderliness. On a positive note, they generally demonstrate genuine concern for the well-being of others, and it's uncommon to find a Fox child who is cruel or unkind. From an early age, they frequently display empathy and a willingness to assist and support others. A Fox child is clever and curious, with a natural inquisitiveness and quick wit. They are resourceful problem-solvers, often finding creative solutions to challenges. Social and charming, they make friends easily and enjoy engaging in playful activities. Their adaptable nature helps them thrive in various environments and situations.

The Fox Friend

Foxes are known for their quick wit and sharp intellect, often offering insightful conversation perspectives. This makes them engaging and entertaining friends who can effortlessly lighten the mood and provide thoughtful advice. Fox friends are highly adaptable and versatile, navigating different social situations easily. They thrive in diverse groups, appreciating the variety of personalities and viewpoints. This adaptability also means they are excellent at mediating conflicts, using their diplomatic skills to resolve disputes and maintain harmony within the group. Loyal and supportive, Fox friends are always there when needed, offering a listening ear and practical solutions to problems. They are resourceful and innovative, often contributing creative ideas to help their friends escape tricky situations. Their ability to think outside the box is an asset, especially when facing challenges or planning exciting activities. Charming and sociable, Fox friends enjoy making connections and have a knack for networking. They are the glue that holds social groups together, ensuring everyone feels included and valued. Their natural curiosity leads them to explore new interests and experiences, and they often invite their friends to share the adventure. This adventurous spirit keeps their friendships dynamic and full of fun. However, their playful nature can sometimes be mistaken for inconsistency. While they enjoy lighthearted fun, they also deeply value genuine connections and loyalty. Fox friends may occasionally need reassurance that their loyalty and support are reciprocated. A Fox friend is clever, adaptable, and charming. They are loyal and supportive, with a talent for resolving conflicts and maintaining harmony. Their adventurous spirit and sociable nature make them delightful and dependable companions, enriching the lives of those around them.

The Fox Partner

A Fox partner is engaging, resourceful, and caring, making them both exciting and reliable companions. Fox partners are known for their sharp intellect and quick wit. They have a natural ability to think on their feet and devise clever solutions to problems. This makes them excellent conversationalists who stimulate and entertain their partner intellectually. One of the defining traits of a Fox partner is their adaptability. They are highly flexible and can adjust to changing circumstances with ease. Whether it's a sudden change in plans or a new challenge, they handle it ingeniously. This adaptability makes them supportive partners who can navigate life's ups and downs without getting flustered, providing a sense of stability and confidence in the relationship. While Fox partners are known for their playful and fun-loving nature, they also possess a deep and introspective side. They can have meaningful, heartfelt conversations, offering profound insights and emotional support. This balance of playfulness and depth ensures that the relationship is enjoyable and deeply fulfilling.

Fox partners possess a natural charm that draws people to them. They are sociable and enjoy interacting with others, often being the life of the party. This charisma helps them build strong social networks, and they love introducing their partner to new people and experiences. Their outgoing nature ensures the relationship remains vibrant and socially enriching, with plenty of shared adventures and memorable moments. Despite their playful and sociable demeanor, Fox partners are loyal and supportive. They value their relationships and are committed to their partner's happiness and well-being. They always offer a listening ear, practical advice, or a shoulder to lean on during tough times.

Fox partners are incredibly resourceful and know how to find creative solutions to problems. Whether planning a surprise date or tackling a difficult situation, they use their ingenuity to devise unique and effective approaches. This resourcefulness makes them dependable partners who can handle challenges with confidence and flair, adding an element of excitement and unpredictability to the relationship. With a natural curiosity and love for adventure, Fox partners are always eager to explore new horizons. They enjoy trying new activities, visiting new places, and learning new things, and they often encourage their partner to join them in these adventures. This adventurous spirit keeps the relationship dynamic and fresh, fostering shared growth and discovery.

In times of conflict, Fox partners find common ground. They approach conflicts calmly and rationally, striving to understand their partner's perspective and resolve issues amicably. Their ability to communicate effectively and empathetically helps maintain harmony and strengthen the relationship.

ACKNOWLEDGMENTS

I would like to thank the following people for their invaluable help: Yvan Cartwright for his fantastic IT support; my researchers Helena Brooks, Jade Attridge, Sally Evans, and Dave Moore; and Jon Graham, Manzanita Carpenter Sanz, Kelly Bowen, Albo Sudekum, and all the rest of the team at Inner Traditions.

NOTES

NEW EVIDENCE FOR ASTROLOGY

1. Gauquelin and Gauquelin, *American Charts.*
2. Kreitzman and Foster, *Seasons of Life.*
3. Shackelford, *Chronobiology*, vol. 1.
4. Shackelford, *Chronobiology*, vol. 2.
5. Tendler et al., "Hormone Seasonality."
6. Petraglia et al., *Hormones and Pregnancy.*
7. Tendler et al., "Hormone Seasonality."

THE ORIGINAL ZODIAC

1. Soliman, "Turtle."
2. Sun and Kistemaker, *Chinese Sky.*
3. Milbrath, *Star Gods.*
4. Beck, *Ancient Astrology.*
5. Kriwaczek, *Babylon.*
6. Koch-Westenholz, *Mesopotamian Astrology.*
7. Powell, *Zodiac.*
8. Koch-Westenholz, *Mesopotamian Astrology.*
9. Hunger et al., *Archives of Assyria.*
10. Berger, "Obliquity and Precession."
11. Hilton, "Precession and the Ecliptic."
12. Dehant and Mathews, *Precession, Nutation, and Wobble.*

13. Northedge and Kennet, *Archaeological Atlas.*
14. Collins, *Göbekli Tepe.*
15. Newman, *Megaliths.*
16. Dalley, *Mesopotamia Creation.*
17. Bottéro and Fagan, *Religion in Mesopotamia.*

BIBLIOGRAPHY

Beck, Roger. *A Brief History of Ancient Astrology*. Hoboken, NJ: Wiley-Blackwell, 2006.

Berger, A. L. "Obliquity and Precession for the Last 5,000,000 Years." *Astronomy and Astrophysics* 51, no. 1 (1976).

Bottéro, Jean, and T. L. Fagan, trans. *Religion in Ancient Mesopotamia*. Chicago, IL: University of Chicago Press, 2004.

Collins, Andrew. *Göbekli Tepe: Genesis of the Gods: The Temple of the Watchers and the Discovery of Eden*. Rochester, VT: Bear & Company, 2014.

Dalley, Stephanie, trans. *Myths from Mesopotamia Creation—The Flood, Gilgamesh, and Others*. Oxford, UK: Oxford University Press, 2008.

Dehant, V., and P. M. Mathews. *Precession, Nutation, and Wobble of the Earth*. Cambridge, UK: Cambridge University Press, 2015.

Gauquelin, Francoise, and Michel Gauquelin. *Gauquelin Book of American Charts*. Washington, DC: ACS Publications, 1988.

Hilton, J. L., et al. "Report of the International Astronomical Union Division I Working Group on Precession and the Ecliptic." *Celestial Mechanics and Dynamical Astronomy* no. 94, Issue 3 (2006).

Hunger, H., S. Parpolaed, and J. Reade. *State Archives of Assyria: Astrological Reports to Assyrian Kings*. Helsinki, Finland: Helsinki University Press, 1992.

Koch-Westenholz, Ulla. *Mesopotamian Astrology: An Introduction to Babylonian and Assyrian Celestial Divination.* Copenhagen, Denmark: Museum Tusculanum Press, 1995.

Kreitzman, Leon, and Russell Foster. *Seasons of Life: The Biological Rhythms that Enable Living Things to Thrive and Survive.* London, UK: Profile Books, 2010.

Kriwaczek, Paul. *Babylon: Mesopotamia and the Birth of Civilization.* London, UK: Atlantic Books, 2014.

Milbrath, Susan. *Star Gods of the Maya: Astronomy in Art, Folklore, and Calendars.* Austin, TX: University of Texas Press, 2000.

Newman, Hugh. *Göbekli Tepe and Karahan Tepe: The World's First Megaliths.* Bury St. Edmunds, UK: Wooden Books, 2023.

Northedge, A., and D. Kennet. *Samarra Studies II: Archaeological Atlas of Samarra.* London, UK: The British Institute for the Study of Iraq, 2015.

Petraglia, Felice, Mariarosaria Di Tommaso, and Federico Mecacci, eds. *Hormones and Pregnancy: Basic Science and Clinical Implications.* Cambridge, UK: Cambridge University Press, 2022.

Powell, Robert. *History of the Zodiac.* London, UK: Sophia Foundation Press, 2017.

Shackelford, Jole. *An Introduction to the History of Chronobiology.* Volume 1: *Biological Rhythms Emerge as a Subject of Scientific Research.* Pittsburgh, PA: University of Pittsburgh Press, 2022.

———. *An Introduction to the History of Chronobiology.* Volume 2: *Biological Rhythms in Animals and Humans.* Pittsburgh, PA: University of Pittsburgh Press, 2022.

Soliman, Wael Sayed. "Turtle, the Mysterious of the Sky." *International Journal of Heritage, Tourism and Hospitality* 14, no. 2 (2020).

Sun, Xiaochun, and Jacob Kistemaker. *The Chinese Sky During the Han: Constellating Stars and Society.* Leiden, Netherlands: Brill, 1997.

Tendler, Avichai, Alon Bar, Netta Mendelsohn-Cohen, et al. "Hormone Seasonality in Medical Records Suggests Circannual Endocrine Circuits." *Proceedings of the National Academy of Sciences*: 118, no. 7 (2021).

BOOKS OF RELATED INTEREST

The Mystery of Doggerland
Atlantis in the North Sea
by Graham Phillips

Exploring the latest archaeological findings and recent scientific analysis of Doggerland's underwater remains in the North Sea, Graham Phillips shows that this ancient culture had sophisticated technology and advanced medical knowledge. He also reveals how the survivors of the destruction of Doggerland sailed to the British Isles and established the megalithic culture that built Stonehenge.

Aspects in Astrology
A Guide to Understanding
Planetary Relationships in the Horoscope
by Sue Tompkins

Aspects—the relationships between the stars and planets—are an essential piece when it comes to interpreting the destiny of an individual from astrological information. Tompkins provides both the novice and the experienced astrologer the evidence and concrete methods needed to grasp the vast knowledge offered to us by our horoscope.

Astrology in Ancient Mesopotamia
The Science of Omens and the Knowledge of the Heavens
by Michael Baigent

Among the many artifacts excavated from King Ashurbanipal's library in Nineveh were tablets documenting the development of Mesopotamian astrology, now recognized as the earliest astrological science. Michael Baigent (*Holy Blood, Holy Grail*) traces the transmission of this knowledge over the centuries from Mesopotamia, through Egypt and Florence, to modern times.